NORTH ARKANSAS COLLEGE LIBRARY
1515 Pioneer Drive
Harrison, AR   72601

WITHDRAWN

D1512286

At Issue

Women in Islam

Other Books in the At Issue Series:

At Issue

Women in Islam

Diane Andrews Henningfeld, Book Editor

GREENHAVEN PRESS
A part of Gale, Cengage Learning

GALE
CENGAGE Learning™

Detroit • New York • San Francisco • New Haven, Conn • Waterville, Maine • London

HQ
1170
. W577
2011

GALE
CENGAGE Learning·

Christine Nasso, *Publisher*
Elizabeth Des Chenes, *Managing Editor*

© 2011 Greenhaven Press, a part of Gale, Cengage Learning.

Gale and Greenhaven Press are registered trademarks used herein under license.

For more information, contact:
Greenhaven Press
27500 Drake Rd.
Farmington Hills, MI 48331-3535
Or you can visit our Internet site at gale.cengage.com

ALL RIGHTS RESERVED.
No part of this work covered by the copyright herein may be reproduced, transmitted, stored, or used in any form or by any means graphic, electronic, or mechanical, including but not limited to photocopying, recording, scanning, digitizing, taping, Web distribution, information networks, or information storage and retrieval systems, except as permitted under Section 107 or 108 of the 1976 United States Copyright Act, without the prior written permission of the publisher.

For product information and technology assistance, contact us at

Gale Customer Support, 1-800-877-4253
For permission to use material from this text or product, submit all requests online at www.cengage.com/permissions.

Further permissions questions can be e-mailed to permissionrequest@cengage.com.

Articles in Greenhaven Press anthologies are often edited for length to meet page requirements. In addition, original titles of these works are changed to clearly present the main thesis and to explicitly indicate the author's opinion. Every effort is made to ensure that Greenhaven Press accurately reflects the original intent of the authors. Every effort has been made to trace the owners of copyrighted material.

Cover Image created by Andrew Judd/© 1999–2009 Masterfile Corporation. All rights reserved.

LIBRARY OF CONGRESS CATALOGING-IN-PUBLICATION DATA

Women in Islam / Diane Andrews Henningfeld, book editor.
    p. cm. -- (At issue)
    Includes bibliographical references and index.
    ISBN 978-0-7377-4904-5 (hardcover) -- ISBN 978-0-7377-4905-2 (pbk.)
    1. Muslim women--Juvenile literature. 2. Muslim women--Conduct of life-- Juvenile literature. 3. Women--Religious aspects--Juvenile literature. I. Henningfeld, Diane Andrews.
    HQ1170.W577 2010
    305.48'697--dc22
                                                                    2010017203

Printed in the United States of America
1 2 3 4 5 6 7 14 13 12 11 10

Contents

Introduction

One of the most hotly debated topics concerning the interface between Islam and the Western world is the institution of sharia law in non-Muslim majority countries. For women in particular, the growing tendency in some Western nations to allow or include sharia courts to operate has serious implications.

Sharia is the Islamic legal code, and according to the Council of Foreign Relations' March 23, 2009 publication "Islam: Governing Under Sharia," by Lauren Vriens, "Sharia guides all aspects of Muslim life including daily routines, familial and religious obligations, and financial dealings." Sharia is based on the hadith, a collection of sayings and narratives about the Prophet Muhammad's life; the Qur'an, the Muslim holy book; the opinions of Islamic scholars; and the consensus of the community, according to Vriens.

In Western communities, sharia is best known for the severity of its punishment of criminal offenses. In Muslim countries that use sharia courts exclusively, flogging, caning, stoning, amputation of hands, and execution are commonly used as punishments for a variety of offenses. Indeed, according to Vriens, "Many majority Muslim countries have a dual system in which the government is secular but Muslims can choose to bring familial and financial disputes to sharia courts." Cases arising from marriage, divorce, and female behavior are nearly always handled by sharia courts, and it is virtually impossible for a woman in a Muslim country to have access to secular courts for the resolution of domestic issues.

The dual system is making its presence felt in Western countries with large Muslim populations. The United Kingdom, for example, officially granted sharia courts the power to rule on Muslim civil cases, according to Abul Taher, writing in the September 14, 2008 edition of *The Sunday Times*

(London). The courts are set up as arbitration tribunals, and their rulings "are binding in law, provided that both parties in the dispute agree to give it the power to rule on their case." The sharia courts in the United Kingdom have handled cases that include marriage, divorce, domestic violence, and inheritance, as well as some assault cases.

Sharia law is controversial because it imposes differing conditions for men and women in several areas. According to Dipesh Gadher, Abul Taher, and Christopher Morgan writing in the February 2008 edition of *The Sunday Times*, "Under sharia it is usually the husband who initiates divorce proceedings—and, in theory, can end a marriage by saying 'I divorce thee' . . . on three separation occasions. Women can apply to a sharia court for divorce only if they are able to provide a legitimate reason, such as being the victim of domestic abuse." Although there is debate among Qur'anic scholars over how divorce should be handled, in practice, women are not able to initiate a divorce proceeding without their husband's consent, and according to sharia law, a man's testimony is worth twice the testimony of a woman. Although a woman can expect to recover her dowry, or the amount paid by her family to her husband's family, on divorce, sharia does not call for husbands to provide any support (such as alimony) for women after divorce. Likewise, sharia calls for male heirs to receive larger inheritances than female heirs. Theoretically, the discrepancy in inheritance is due to a man's responsibility for providing for his immediate and extended family. Thus, a man's inheritance is likely to be distributed among the members of his family or used for their support. A woman, on the other hand, has, in theory, less need of an inheritance as she supposedly controls her dowry, money that can serve as her discretionary income.

There is fear that widespread acceptance of sharia among Muslim communities in the United Kingdom will make it increasingly difficult for Muslim women growing up in the country to be aware of the rights granted to them by the British constitution. Furthermore, it is difficult to determine if women who agree to have their cases heard by the sharia court do so voluntarily, or if they are being forced to choose the sharia court over the secular, civil courts under pressure from their families.

Dalia Mogahed, an adviser to U.S. president Barack Obama, however, believes that most women worldwide support sharia courts. Andrew Gilligan, writing in the October 9, 2009 edition of *The Daily Telegraph* reports that Mogahed said the following on a British television show: "'I think the reason so many women support sharia is because they have a very different understanding of sharia than the common perception in Western media. The majority of women around the world associate gender justice, or justice for women, with sharia compliance.'" Hamid Tawfik, writing in the December 10, 2009 edition of *Newsmax*, offers a radically different opinion about the possibility of sharia courts operating in the United States. He writes, "Accepting the idea that our constitutional laws can be broken to accommodate Shariah and satisfy the Muslim population actually can open the gate for both discrimination against non-Muslims and the practice of many unconstitutional and inhumane laws."

The institution of sharia law also raises other concerns, including polygamy, in countries such as the United Kingdom, where it is considered a crime. According to Gadher et al., a sharia court in Leyton ruled that a man who had a wife in the United Kingdom but had "tired of her" could marry a second wife in Pakistan and subsequently bring her to the United Kingdom. The court ruled "he should remain married and treat them both equally." In other words, the sharia court encouraged the man to engage in polygamy in a country where the practice is clearly illegal.

The issue of sharia law illustrates a most difficult question: Does sharia adequately protect women's rights while protecting religious freedom? Edna Fernandes, writing in the July 4,

2009 edition of the *Mail Online* summarizes thus: "Sharia law in Britain is here to stay and perhaps even spread. But it's a perilous tightrope we tread—the line between multicultural tolerance and protecting the rights of the individual."

Sharia law is just one of the many challenges faced by women in Islam. Issues of dress, sexuality, justice, rights, and violence all affect how Muslim women live their lives, and these issues form the heart of the debate in the viewpoints that follow.

NORTH ARKANSAS COLLEGE LIBRARY
1515 Pioneer Drive
Harrison, AR 72601

1

Women in Islam: An Overview

Priscilla Offenhauer

Priscilla Offenhauer is a senior research analyst for the Library of Congress.

The Western view of Muslim women draws heavily on the Middle East and North Africa region, even though this region is home to only 20 percent of the world Muslim population. The patriarchal Islamic gender system affects the lives of many Muslim women in that it underpins the legal systems of many countries. Although gender-based inequality continues, women have made strides in educational levels and careers. Many Muslim women in Islamic countries have also gained the right to vote and engage in political activism.

More than half a billion of the women in the world are Muslim. They are concentrated in approximately 45 Muslim-majority countries in a broad belt from Senegal to the Philippines, with the largest number on the South Asian subcontinent. The most populous single Muslim-majority nation is Indonesia.

• Monolithic stereotypes of Muslim women have long prevailed in the West, distorting the enormous interregional, intraregional, and class variations in their circumstances and status.

• Serious social scientific scholarship on women worldwide was scarce until the 1970s. Since then the study of women, including Muslim women, has exploded. The social science literature on Muslim women is now voluminous and growing.

Priscilla Offenhauer, *Women in Islamic Societies: A Selected Review of Social Scientific Literature*, Washington, DC: Library of Congress, 2005.

• The Western understanding of Muslim women remains unduly influenced by evidence from a single region. The social science scholarship most familiar to the West about Muslim women focuses disproportionately on the Middle East and North Africa region (MENA). Often seen as the land of Muslims par excellence, MENA is home to fewer than 20 percent of the world's Muslims.

Muslim Women and Patriarchy

• Women in Muslim societies and communities face gender-based inequalities associated with the so-called "patriarchal gender system." Aspects of this originally pre-capitalist system persist in rural areas across a wide swath of lands, both Muslim and non-Muslim, from East Asia to North Africa. The system, regardless of religion, features kin-based extended families, male domination, early marriage (and consequent high fertility), restrictive codes of female behavior, the linkage of family honor with female virtue, and occasionally, polygamous family structure. In Muslim areas, veiling and sex-segregation form part of the gender system.

• Most current scholarship rejects the idea that the Islamic religion is the primary determinant of the status and conditions of Muslim women. Because of the wide variation in Muslim women's status and conditions, researchers typically attribute more causal salience to determining factors that themselves vary across nations and regions. To account for the variable situations of Muslim women, scholars cite as causal factors, for example, variations in the economic structures and strategies of nations, or variations in the preexisting cultural value patterns of a given locale.

• The sacred writings of Islam, like those of the other Abrahamic faiths—Christianity and Judaism—have been interpreted in ways that support patriarchal social relations. Until the last two decades, Western observers of the plight of Muslim women have portrayed Islam as uniquely patriarchal and incompatible with women's equality. Most scholars now see Islam as no more inherently misogynist than the other major monotheistic traditions.

• Many cultural practices associated with Islam and criticized as oppressive to women are misidentified as "Islamic." Controversial or egregious practices such as female circumcision, polygamy, early marriage, and honor killings are not limited to Muslim populations, and among Muslims such practices are geographically specific or otherwise far from universal.

Women's Legal Position and Rights

• The legal systems under which women live in Muslim countries are mostly dual systems. They consist, on the one hand, of civil law, which is indebted to Western legal systems, and on the other hand, of family or personal status law, which is mainly built upon Sharia, Islamic religious-based law. The civil law as well as the constitutions of many Muslim states provide for equal rights between women and men. However, Islamic family law as variously manifested in Muslim nations poses obstacles to women's equality.

• Islamic family law, which addresses marriage, divorce, child custody, and inheritance, has long been a target for reform. Many state elites have pressed for family law reform to further state interests by removing hindrances to women's full participation in the labor force and politics.

• Reforms of family law often have been limited by the state's perceived need to appease conservative social elements and, since the 1970s, growing Islamist movements. Islamist movements, sometimes through outright state takeover, as in Iran, occasionally have succeeded in rolling back "women-friendly" reforms previously achieved.

• Family law reforms continue, often thanks to the pressure of proliferating groups of Muslim activists for women rights. In 2004, a major success was the overhaul of conservative family law in Morocco, which now boasts a relatively progressive system.

• In many Muslim states, the substance of family law and its actual implementation differ in ways that somewhat mitigate the gender imbalance of the laws on the books. Women are able and sometimes officially encouraged to exploit rules and loopholes to circumvent discriminatory provisions in the law. Women can, for example, write clauses into marriage contracts that make taking another wife grounds for divorce and for post-divorce division of marital assets. A growing form of feminist activism at present aims to educate women about such strategies and available loopholes.

Viewed in terms of large-scale statistical indicators, Muslim women are becoming ever more like other women.

Health and Education

• Whatever hindrances to equality Muslim legal systems pose for women, Muslim women across all regions have made rapid progress in recent decades in a number of statistically measurable aspects of life, notably education and health. In these areas, Muslim nations have significantly reduced both gender gaps and the formerly wide differences in average attainment between Muslim and non-Muslim societies. In education, for example, a generation ago women in MENA had among the lowest levels of education in the world. MENA females now have achieved parity with males at some levels of schooling.

• Macro-level statistics also show a rapid reduction in Muslim and non-Muslim differences in reproduction-related behaviors. In the recent past, Muslim women exhibited comparatively high rates of fertility and low rates of contraception use. They now are participating in the worldwide trend of declining fertility. In some cases, such as in Iran, they have attained below-replacement fertility. Iran, in fact, effected the most rapid demographic transition ever seen.

• Viewed in terms of large-scale statistical indicators, Muslim women are becoming ever more like other women. This fact undercuts the assumption that "Islam" would inhibit Muslim women's participation in such worldwide trends as declining childbearing. On average, broad social and economic forces for change override whatever special influence Islam might have.

Marriage, Family, Household, and Everyday Life

• In the sphere of the family, macro-level statistics indicate a shift to a nuclear family from a pattern of extended family and multi-generational households. Statistics also indicate that Muslims are delaying marriage and increasing their rate of non-marriage. Such shifts spell erosion of the traditional kinship-based patriarchal family, which persists as an ideal among conservatives.

• Caught between the traditional patriarchal family model and an egalitarian nuclear model, today's Muslim families have been called "neopatriarchal." They continue to feature intra-familial gender-based inequality.

• Scholarship within the last decade has begun to address the darkest aspects of such familial gender-based inequality, including the hitherto taboo topics of domestic violence, honor killings, and female circumcision. Such charged issues have figured prominently on the agendas of women's rights advocates in Muslim communities since the Fourth World Conference on Women in Beijing in 1995.

Muslim Women and Work

• Establishing the levels of the labor force participation of Muslim women is a challenge to researchers because a high proportion of women's paid work, as in all developing economies, occurs in the informal economy.

• In at least one heavily Muslim region, namely, MENA, female labor force participation appears to be exceptionally low, although growing. In other Muslim-majority lands, for example, Southeast Asia, it is high.

• The levels of Muslim women's participation in the paid labor force are best explained by a particular economy's development strategy and consequent need for female labor, rather than by, for example, religious ideology or cultural beliefs in male breadwinner/female-homemaker roles. In the oil-boom years prior to the mid-1980s, the oil-centered economies of MENA did not require female labor in order to grow. Thus, oil-rich nations such as Saudi Arabia had few women in the labor force. By contrast, Muslim counties that sought to develop through labor-intensive industrial production, such as Tunisia, Malaysia, or Indonesia, feature high female labor force participation.

Although Muslim women are underrepresented in formal politics, their activism within Muslim states for the advancement of women's rights and interests is widespread and growing.

• The globalization of the past quarter century—i.e., the increasing international integration of markets in the global capitalist economy—is a fundamental factor in the evolving role of women in Muslim societies, as in others.

• Globalization increased economic and job insecurity and thus the need for more than one breadwinner in a family. At the same time, in many national economies, globalization has reduced the proportion of formal sector employment, which was in any case out of reach for many Muslim women. Globalization also has prompted the withdrawal of the state from service provision, thereby increasing women's family burdens. The effect of globalization on Muslim women thus often has been increased hardship. At the same time, many women have reported an enhanced sense of empowerment as a result of their enlarged public role and earnings.

Women in Muslim States and Politics

• Women have gained basic political rights—the right to vote and to stand for office—in almost all Muslim-majority states, with the last major holdouts, Kuwait and Saudi Arabia, on the verge of joining the others. Despite having such rights, Muslim women, like women worldwide, are underrepresented in high office and legislatures. However, a number of Muslim countries outside of MENA have . . . women in high office in numbers that exceed world averages. Such cases of above-average office-holding generally reflect quota systems and/or the power of family ties in politics.

• Although Muslim women are underrepresented in formal politics, their activism within Muslim states for the advancement of women's rights and interests is widespread and growing. Advocacy and activist groups have proliferated, exhibiting great variety in their political complexion, in their avowal of religious commitment, and in the radicalism of their demands for change.

• In the 1990s, secular feminists and so-called Islamic feminists, formerly at odds, achieved some rapprochement. Secular feminists now recognize value in the other camp's preoccupation with providing woman-friendly "rereadings" of Islam's sacred texts. Justifying feminist activism in Islamic terms shields feminist demands from the charge that they are alien Western impositions. Islamic feminists increasingly see Islamic precepts and universal (e.g., United Nations) articulations of human/women's rights as compatible.

• A significant development for Muslim women's rights activists in the past decade has been the growth of transnational networks, such as Women Living Under Muslim Laws and Sisters in Islam. Exploiting the revolution in communications, these networks advocate legal reform and organize resistance to Islamist threats to women's progress.

2

Muslim Women Should Not Be Stereotyped

Mona Eltahawy

Mona Eltahawy is a syndicated columnist and international speaker on Middle Eastern and Muslim affairs.

The President of the United States and other world leaders should realize that Muslim women are more than the headscarves some of them choose to wear. More important issues include the right to divorce, the fight against domestic violence, and fighting forced marriages. Rather than supporting the right to wear a headscarf, leaders should be working to support choice in the matter. To do otherwise is to perpetuate stereotypes.

When President Barack Obama said he wanted to address women's rights during his speech to Muslims last week, [June 2009] I said a prayer to the God of the Torah, the Bible and the Quran [the Islamic sacred book, believed to be the word of God as Sharia Law]: please don't let him fall into the trap of headscarves and hymens.

The conversation about Muslim women too often revolves around what's on our heads and what's between our legs. My hopes were high that Obama—surrounded by powerful women at home and work—would avoid that pitfall of too many Muslims and non-Muslims alike.

Confession: I'm utterly under Obama's charm, which worries this woman from the Middle East, where we've had our

Mona Eltahawy, "Headscarves and Hymens," The Huffington Post, June 16, 2009. Reproduced by permission of the author.

share of charismatic men with disarming oratory skills. I check that charm with higher expectations of this entirely different creature of president: cosmopolitan, has lived abroad, has family all over the globe. I know Obama knows better than George W. Bush.

Muslim Women Fight Against Misogyny

Which is why I was distraught that Obama had such low expectations for Muslim women. The 13 or so lines dedicated to us focused on headscarves and education, a bland and stereotypical view of Muslim women that ignored the courageous creativity of so many fighting against misogyny and male-dominated interpretations of my religion.

I met many such women—some in headscarves, many not—in Kuala Lumpur earlier this year at the launch of Musawah, a global movement for justice and equality in the Muslim family. Panel discussions and dinner talk among the 250 activists and scholars from 47 countries were heated, but not about headscarves or education.

We had much heavier issues on our minds—like a woman's right to initiate divorce, how to protect women against clerics who say Islam gives a husband the right to beat his wife, fighting forced marriage. In other words, wrestling Islam back from the men who use it against us.

And the conversation will continue when I return to Kuala Lumpur in July for the second gathering of WISE—Women's Islamic Initiative in Spirituality and Equity—which has on its agenda [to] launch the first global Muslim women's consultative council (think of a group of women ready to issue fatwas or religious edicts) as a way of acknowledging Muslim women's hunger for religious authority.

As Muslim women, we're not waiting for the president of the United States to open doors for us or to fight our fights. The Bush administration and its "we'll liberate you by invading your countries" doctrine is [behind us, thankfully]. It is up to us to fight for our rights inside our communities.

How President Barack Obama Can Help

But there are several ways the president of the United States can help. He can listen to the diverse voices of Muslim women and not just the most conservative interpretation of Islam that some hear out of misguided "cultural sensitivity."

It is not culturally sensitive for example to stay silent when an eight-year-old girl is forced into marriage as was reported from Saudi Arabia last year. It is criminally unjust. It is invariably men who define "culture" and invariably women and girls who bear its brunt.

By seeing our diversity, the president of the United States can avoid the headscarf conundrum. I'm glad he avoided hymens, and it was good to hear Obama make clear to his Muslim audience that the U.S. government had gone to court to protect Muslim women's right to wear headscarves. Surely it should be about choice.

How I wish Obama had paid homage to the brave girls and women of [Afghanistan] who risk life and limb to learn while the Taliban's misogyny fights to imprison them at home.

So why not support choice for women everywhere, even in Muslim-majority countries? Here's where it gets complicated and confusing. In Egypt, which played host to Obama's speech, women have gone to court and lost in their fight for their right to wear headscarves as anchors on state-run television channels and as flight attendants on state-owned Egypt Air.

In Saudi Arabia, Obama's first port of call during last week's [June, 2009] trip, girls and women have no choice but to cover up or suffer the cruelty of the morality police who in

2002 barred girls from fleeing their burning school building because they weren't wearing headscarves. Fifteen girls burned to death.

In Muslim-majority Turkey—the first Muslim country Obama visited since taking office—women are barred from wearing headscarves on state-run university campuses and in government buildings.

Education Is a Basic Right

When it comes to education, surely the most basic right for girls and women everywhere, again it's complicated. In Saudi Arabia—recognized as one of the worst violators of women's rights—women outnumber men on university campuses and yet are treated like minors who need a male guardian's permission to do the most basic things.

Afghanistan is the primary battleground for female education. How I wish Obama had paid homage to the brave girls and women of that country who risk life and limb to learn while the Taliban's misogyny fights to imprison them at home. In May [2009], 90 Afghan girls were hospitalized—with five slipping briefly into comas—after the Taliban staged the third poison gas attack in as many weeks on girls' schools.

I wish Obama had promised those girls and women that he would not sacrifice their rights if the U.S. talks to the Taliban as has been suggested as a way to curb fighting in Afghanistan.

I wish Muslim women didn't need their own part in the speech. Many wondered whether Obama would take the safe route and avoid women's rights. But that would have given a free pass to the denial and defensiveness of too many Muslims about the abuse of girls and women committed in the name of our religion.

But I urge Obama to avoid a free pass to oversimplified stereotypes. He's too smart—and charming—for that.

NORTH ARKANSAS COLLEGE LIBRARY
1515 Pioneer Drive
Harrison, AR 72601

3

Muslim Women Need Their Rights to Be Recognized

Katha Pollitt

Katha Pollitt writes the "Subject to Debate" column for The Nation *magazine.*

Many feminists believe that President Barack Obama's June 2009 speech spent too little time on the issue of rights for women, and particularly the rights of Muslim women in countries like Saudi Arabia. Too many Westerners fail to recognize that Muslim women are actively struggling for their rights in many countries. While the banning of the burqa in France is being hailed by some feminists and a French Muslim women's group, the ban will not secure the basic human rights Muslim women should have.

I thought President Obama's Cairo speech [June 2009] was basically fine: begin anew, extend the hand, reject "crude stereotypes" all around, turn the page on the Christian triumphalism of the Bush years. But there's no denying that the section on women's rights was rather minimal, just three paragraphs, compared with his long discourse on Israel and Palestine; and to my American ears its priorities were a bit odd. You would think the biggest issue for Muslim women is that someone is preventing them from wearing a headscarf: "The US government has gone to court to protect the right of women and girls to wear the hijab [a head scarf worn by

Katha Pollitt, "Muslim Women's Rights, Continued," *The Nation*, June 24, 2009. Copyright © 2009 by The Nation Magazine/The Nation Company, Inc. Reproduced by permission.

Muslim women, concealing hair and neck; often includes a face veil] and to punish those who would deny it," he said. "I reject the view of some in the West that a woman who chooses to cover her hair is somehow less equal." Fair enough, but that woman is choosing. What about Saudi or Iranian women, who are forced by law to cover? Obama noted that countries where women are well educated tend to be more prosperous and promised American aid for women's literacy and micro-loans. These are both good things, especially in desperately poor and underdeveloped countries like Afghanistan; but face it, to become full participants in modern societies, women need more than a grade school education and a sewing machine. They need their rights. In fact, some Muslim countries, like Iran, Saudi Arabia and the Gulf states, already have large numbers of highly educated women—in Iran, as in America, more young women go to college than men. But those women are prevented from working to their capacity, or even at all, by religiously motivated sex discrimination. In Saudi Arabia, women can't even work in lingerie stores. By a quirk of the gender-apartheid regulations, only men can sell ladies' underwear. So much for "modesty": when there's money to be made from women, you can be sure the theocrats will figure out a reason that God wants it to go into men's pockets.

A Call for Full Civil Rights for Muslim Women

I can see why Obama didn't issue a ringing call for full civil rights for Muslim women: an end to stoning and lashings and female genital mutilation, to forced marriage and child marriage, to family law that enshrines male privilege, the valuing of women's testimony in court as half that of a man's and the scandalous laws that punish as unchaste those rape victims who lack four witnesses—male witnesses, of course—to the crime. Such a statement would have backfired; it would have allowed traditionalists and theocrats to pose as anti-imperialists, defenders of culture and religion against the impious West. Moreover, as he properly noted, women struggle for their rights all over the world, not just under Islam. But I can also see why some feminists were disappointed not to get more of a shout-out. "It seems that Mr. Obama is attempting to build political bridges by taking a more socially conservative stance, a common—but mistaken—tack in the struggle against fundamentalism and terrorism," writes Algerian-American human rights lawyer Karima Bennoune on the blog Europe: Solidaire Sans Frontières. "This may also be the reason that the President felt compelled to stress his respect for 'women who choose to live their lives in traditional roles,' rather than, say, referencing the critical struggles of the Egyptian women's movement. Welcome to the new cultural relativism. We're not going to deal with human rights problems in your part of the world, because we want your extremists to stop blowing us up."

The energetic and massive participation of women in the [Iranian] street demonstrations [is] only surprising if you think Muslim women really are as weak and passive as the mullahs imagine.

The title of Bennoune's article, "The Religionizing of Politics," points to another problem: the tendency in the West to treat majority-Muslim countries as a single cohesive entity—"the Muslim world"—rather than as Asian, African and Middle Eastern nations that are as different from one another as the majority-Christian lands of Britain and Mexico. The term itself promotes the view that Islam *tout court* [in short] is what these countries are all about, thus marginalizing other ways of understanding them and rendering invisible the non-Muslims and seculars who live there.

Muslim Women Are Strong and Motivated

The current election struggle in Iran came as a big surprise to those who take the simplistic view of Muslim nations as our antagonists in a clash of civilizations. Who knew that our arch-enemy, member in good standing of the Axis of Evil, had all these hip young people, these tech-savvy Tweeters, these ordinary citizens eager to go into the streets day after day and risk beatings, arrests and death at the hands of the feared Basij [an Iranian paramilitary, volunteer militia founded by the Ayatollah Khomeini in 1979; they police and enforce Islamic law, sometimes violently]? Who knew it had so many women who, however devout they may or may not be, don't want to be denied ordinary human freedoms in the name of religion, thank you very much? The energetic and massive participation of women in the street demonstrations has received much comment in the Western media, but it's only surprising if you think Muslim women really are as weak and passive as the mullahs imagine.

That impression of Muslim women appears to be shared by [French President] Nicolas Sarkozy, who has thrown his support behind a proposal to ban in France the all-enveloping burqa [a long loose garment covering the entire body with veiled holes for eyes worn in public by many Muslim women] and the niqab [a head scarf that covers a woman's entire face except for the eyes], calling it a "question of women's liberty and dignity." The most vocal French feminists support the ban, as does the French Muslim women's group Ni Putes Ni Soumises (Neither Whores nor Doormats), for whom it's a necessary counterweight to family and community pressures on women. While it may well be true that some of the small number of French women who wear burqas and niqabs are forced into them, it's hard to see how a ban will help liberate them. Instead, it will permit the French to publicly humiliate them and feel good about it, ratify the Islamists' claim that the West is out to get Islam and give more proof that Muslims are unwelcome in France.

4

Western Women in Muslim Lands Lose Their Rights

Judy Bachrach

Judy Bachrach is a contributing editor for Vanity Fair.

Women, including Westerners, who live in Muslim countries are regularly harassed by men and have very few rights. Some Western women who have followed their Muslim husbands to homes in Islamic nations find that they no longer have custody of their children or freedom of movement. If they choose to leave the country, they often have to leave their children behind. In addition, wife beating is common practice, and spousal abuse accepted. In spite of this, the Islamic legal code known as sharia, which often sanctions male dominance, is finding acceptance in countries such as the United Kingdom and Germany.

Every time I despair of the way women are treated in Muslim countries—and the few syllables Western leaders and op-ed columnists expend on their humiliations, mutilations, harassments, and, yes, murders—I turn to the Web site of Mona Eltahawy. Eltahawy spent her formative years in Egypt and Saudi Arabia:

> A couple of years after I stopped visiting, a horrific fire broke out in a school in Mecca, home to the Muslim world's holiest site. Fifteen girls burned to death because morality police standing outside the school wouldn't let them out of the burning building. Why? Because they weren't wearing

Judy Bachrach, "Twice Branded: Western Women in Muslim Lands," *World Affairs*, Summer 2009. Reproduced by permission.

headscarves and abayas [Black loose robes, covering women from head to toe; generally worn in Saudi Arabia. In some countries, the abaya is a burqa.], the black cloaks that girls and women must wear in public in Saudi Arabia.

And here is Eltahawy on a girl's lot in Egypt:

When I was only four years old and still living in Cairo, a man exposed himself to me as I stood on a balcony at my family's, and gestured for me to come down. At 15, I was groped as I was performing the rites of the hajj pilgrimage at Mecca, the holiest site for Muslims. Every part of my body was covered except for my face and hands. I'd never been groped before and burst into tears, but I was too ashamed to explain to my family what had happened.

In a poll of 2,000 Egyptian men, 62 percent admitted harassing women [but insisted that] their advances, however intemperate and offensive to their victims, had after all been provoked by the women themselves.

Sharia Law Is Bad for Women

To anyone who, like me, has lived in a Muslim nation, none of this behavior is either singular or surprising. It is the way men in most Islamic nations prefer things to be. We can talk forever about the nature of culture versus faith: how ancient rites and practices like the circumcision of girls (85 percent of all Egyptian girls have endured this procedure), or the tradition of keeping women ignorant and housebound, can corrupt a religion that never intended for these things to happen.

But it is no coincidence that women who must submit to Sharia law [Islamic law] find themselves in a very bad place, wherever those women and those places happen to be. This includes France, where only last year a court in Lille upheld the right of a Muslim man to hold fast to his faith and annul his marriage when he discovered his bride was not a virgin.

And it includes Germany, where in Berlin in 2005 there were eight murders of young women of Turkish origin, executed by members of their own families. And Australia, where, after a group of unveiled Muslim women were raped, the succinct Mufti Taj al-Din al-Hilali explained away the crime as an attack on "uncovered meat." And it includes the United Kingdom, where Scotland Yard has probed 109 suspicious deaths of women, also likely slaughtered by relatives. Islam is an easy rider: it travels everywhere and often brings with it a lot of baggage.

But let's start with Islam as it affects women in their home countries. Last year, [2008] in a poll of 2,000 Egyptian men, 62 percent admitted harassing women: an activity most of those interviewed insisted was not really their fault as their advances, however intemperate and offensive to their victims, had after all been provoked by the women themselves.

Nor is this sort of harassment confined to Islamic women in Islamic nations. Western women who find themselves in the Middle East come in for their own fair share of daily insults, owing to their double deficit as women and foreigners. Every step outside the home or hotel is an invitation to a carefully directed barrage of verbal assaults, their components familiar and unvarying: vulgar and offensive remarks, leers and snickers, the occasional shove, all accompanied by grins of triumph. When I lived in Egypt, everyone in Cairo avidly watched the television series *Dallas*, and as a result became expert on the sexual habits of American women. And not simply expert, but unrepentantly predatory. After all, these were women whose husbands and brothers would not reflexively massacre those who insulted them. . . .

The Case of Western Women with Muslim Husbands

You don't have to watch a rerun of *Not Without My Daughter*, the harrowing story of Betty Mahmoody, who accompanied her Iranian-born husband back to his native country for what she was assured would be a two-week visit, to understand the possible consequences of such a venture. Mahmoody's eighteen months of virtual house arrest under the vigilant gaze of her doctor husband and his relatives, her escape with her daughter on foot and on horseback are known to us only because her flight was successful. Had it not been, her account would have likely been buried with the rest of her.

Consider the case of Monica Stowers, an American who married a young Saudi she met at the University of Dallas, and with whom she had two children in Texas. In 1983, the young family packed up and moved to Riyadh. There Stowers discovered her husband had another wife he had forgotten to mention. After announcing her decision to return to the U.S. with her small children, she came in for another surprise: Saudi courts gave custody of the children to the father (Stowers was Christian). She went home alone.

Undeterred, in 1990 she returned to Saudi Arabia, gathered her children, and brought them to the U.S. Embassy. At which point, as *The Wall Street Journal* reported well over a decade later, embassy Marines were summoned to expel the family from the premises. The Saudi authorities had an even more effective solution: they arrested Stowers. She left the country. But at 12 years old, her daughter was still languishing in Saudi Arabia, married off to a cousin.

Why Would a Western Woman Move to an Islamic Country?

Why would a Western woman forgo the security and freedom of her home country and relocate with a Muslim husband to an Islamic nation? For an answer, I phoned the feminist author Phyllis Chesler, who has written on the subject. "There is a self-destructiveness in this attraction, a temptation on the part of some women to go to a place where they have servants; or maybe a large extended family that might be wealthier than the one you were born into, or the idea that you yourself might go there and bring change and evolution to a backward country," says Chesler. "You might say there are horrible things that happen to Muslim women in Muslim countries, and that's true. But the Muslim woman expects it, she's used to it—it's terrible but it is something she already knows about. That is not the case with the foreign or Western wife in a Muslim country."

Chesler speaks from authority. Forty-five years ago, she married her college boyfriend, a Muslim from Afghanistan, and followed him home to Kabul. (When I ask why she ever consented to such a radical displacement, there is for the first time in Chesler's narrative a quiet pause. Finally: "It's a question I haven't always been able to answer. We were kindred spirits—also he was the first man I ever slept with. We both loved film, foreign films, and he wanted to go into the field. We were bohemians. I trusted him.")

One Woman's Experience

Here is what happened to her in Kabul—and it's essential to remember this occurred decades before the Taliban made life for women completely intolerable. Chesler's American passport was confiscated at the airport: she never saw it again. Her young "bohemian" husband became, as she notes, "another person": cold and distant, a sometime defender of polygamy (his father, to Chesler's surprise, had three wives) and champion of the veil. Chesler quickly discovered that "Afghans mistrusted foreign wives"—and her walks around the city, invariably barefaced and without the long coat or gloves urged on her by her in-laws, made her the target of lewd advances and crude insults. When she fled to the American embassy, "the Marines would bring me back home every time," she recalls. "I was the wife of a foreign national. I had lost my citizenship."

Her in-laws were deeply unhappy with their son's decision to bring home an American bride. She lived in perpetual fear that she might become, as her husband intended her to be, pregnant. That would have been the end of the narrative, for, as Chesler points out: "You're then going to be trapped in the country you're in forever because you're carrying Muslim property. The child."

When her mother-in-law quietly stopped boiling her drinking water, Chesler developed hepatitis. She weighed 90 pounds on her arrival back in New York City. Her father-in-law, delighted to be rid of her, paid for her ticket home. Because of her experience, the occasional young American woman who is thinking of marrying a Muslim with an urge to return to his own country visits Chesler for advice. And she tells them what she knows: "This man you love will change overnight before your eyes. You will live but you will wish you were dead."

In Turkey, a nation often cited as "moderate," wife beating is so common that almost 85 percent of all male health workers said that violence against women was excusable.

Customs and Mores Regarding Muslim Women

It is, of course, the women who don't get to fly home to New York—or indeed leave any airport without their husbands' consent—who truly deserve international attention. And yet these are the very women our Western politicians, media outlets, and academicians barely acknowledge because, as I was constantly advised by European and American diplomats in both Egypt and also the Sudan when I visited, "We have no right to pass judgment on the customs and mores of other countries."

Here are just a few of those customs and mores: in Turkey, a nation often cited as "moderate," wife beating is so common that 69 percent of all female health workers polled (and almost 85 percent of all male health workers) said that violence against women was in certain instances excusable. In April, a new epidemiological study in the *European Journal of Public Health* revealed that one out of every five homicides in Pakistan is the result of a so-called honor killing. And in Mauritania, the age-old practice of force-feeding young girls—a life-threatening process that is intended to make them round and therefore "marriageable"—has [experienced] a renaissance. Girls as young as five are herded into "fattening farms." Those who resist are tortured.

It was only when our steadfast ally Afghan President Hamid Karzai signed legislation legalizing the rape of his country's wives by their husbands that a powerful Western leader actually expressed a view on the subject. "I think this law is abhorrent," President Barack Obama acknowledged when queried at a press conference in Strasbourg, France. Yet, our president had to be asked about the rape-facilitation law before daring to venture an opinion. Nor is he alone in his bashfulness. All over the world, Western leaders have proven uncommonly demure on the subject of women in Islamic countries. On March 22, 2009, for instance, French foreign minister Bernard Kouchner, the co-founder of Médecins Sans Frontières, and usually no slouch at voicing indignation, found himself in Riyadh, Saudi Arabia, at a formal luncheon. This, on the precise day that a group of 35 Saudi clerics urged their government to ban all women from appearing on television or in newspapers.

What was Kouchner's response to this extraordinary clerical plea? In a press conference, he remarked mildly that he actually had one. He had sat at the luncheon between a Saudi surgeon and a Saudi journalist, both women—and, as he learned, neither was allowed by Saudi law to drive. "I find that bizarre," he concluded. But the restriction of a woman's legitimate movements—her inability to, say, leave the house unaccompanied by a male relation or visit someone else's, her thwarted dreams of driving or braving the heat in garments that allow her skin to breathe—none of these deprivations are really bizarre. They are quite normal.

There are many Muslims who conclude that the Koran permits a man to beat his wife.

What the Koran Says About Women

Accounting for exactly why it is that Islamic countries (or even countries like India, with large Islamic populations) are those that demonstrate the most antipathy toward their female citizens is no straightforward task. On the one hand, Bernard Lewis is correct when he writes that "Islam as a religion and as a culture should not be blamed for the tribal customs of some of the peoples who adopted it." On the other, the Koran [the Islamic sacred book, believed to be the word of God as Sharia Law] is fairly specific about the value of a woman. An Islamic man may accumulate up to four of her kind in marriage—and may divorce any or all of these wives swiftly and without offering a syllable of justification. In court a woman's testimony is worth exactly half of that of a man. In matters of inheritance among siblings, the Koran insists that "the male [must get] twice the share of the female." And finally—although of all the passages this is the one that provokes the most controversy—there are many Muslims who conclude that the Koran permits a man to beat his wife.

"Well, that's Verse 4:34, and it can be interpreted different ways," Hussein Rashid, a professor of religion and political Islam at Hofstra University, demurs. "The verb that is used for hit or beat can also mean 'to break off' or divorce someone." This judicious interpretation of the most incendiary Koranic passage provokes laughter when I repeat it to the Somali-born firebrand Ayaan Hirsi Ali. Allah, she observes, "is absolutely brilliant except when He is speaking about the rights of women—then Allah gets all muddled up, doesn't really mean what He says, and becomes a very confused God." In fact, Hirsi Ali continues, "that the husband has the right to beat his wife *is* in the Koran. That a woman has to dress a certain way is in the Koran, that she must stay in the house is also there. And on it goes."

And everywhere it goes. Sharia travels without a wrinkle on its *burqa* [a long loose garment covering the entire body with veiled holes for eyes worn in public by many Muslim women]. It is no small irony these days that those fortunate countries where women have fought, passionately and at great cost, for equal rights—Germany, France, the United Kingdom, the Netherlands, for instance—have become home to certain Muslim immigrants who continue to violate the rights of women, abetted frequently by both the silence of the authorities and an abashed press. Why this silence? One of the least savory consequences of a colonial past is guilt: an insidious remorse that transmutes itself into a persistent reluctance to criticize publicly those who have now themselves taken on the role of oppressor—even against those who happen to oppress, openly and without shame, within the borders of liberal nations. "You hear people talking about the need to 'respect' other cultures. You want me to respect this awful behavior?" Eltahawy says.

5

Islam Favors Women

Syafa Almirzanah, as told to U.S. Catholic

Syafa Almirzanah is a professor of comparative religion at Islamic University Sunan Kalijaga in Indonesia.

The Qur'an is positive about women and demonstrates that women are equal to men in the sight of Allah. Historically, women were treated very poorly in the Middle East before Islam. The Prophet Muhammad changed women's lot, encouraging them to be educated as his own wives were. Many of the misogynistic teachings of Islam do not come from the Qur'an but from the hadith, traditional sayings. Culture, not religion, is to blame for the mistreatment of women in some Muslim countries. The key to improving the status of women is education.

Syafa Almirzanah, a professor of comparative religion at Islamic University Sunan Kalijaga in Yogyakarta, Indonesia, could have continued her studies anywhere in the Muslim world, but she chose Catholic Theological Union in Chicago. Last spring she became the first Muslim to earn a doctorate from the school.

"Dialogue is, for me, a must," she says. "In my tradition it is the obligation of Muslims to learn from others, to get knowledge from everywhere."

Almirzanah has been active in interreligious dialogue in both her home country of Indonesia and in the United States. She feels comfortable with Catholicism, she says, because of the many similarities between it and Islam.

Syafa Almirzanah, "The Prophet's Daughters: There's Much in Islam That Favors Women, Says This Scholar," *U.S. Catholic*, vol. 74, January 2009, pp. 28–31. Copyright © 2009 by Claretian Publications. Reproduced by permission.

One unfortunate similarity is the way scholars from both traditions have misused faith to repress women. Almirzanah hopes that by learning about the history and theology of Islam—and by participating in interreligious dialogue—Muslims will embrace more female-friendly interpretations of the religion.

In the story of Creation [in the Qur'an], women and men are created from the same cells, so usually scholars say that means that men and women are the same before God.

"I think one of the most important things in dialogue is having the courage to criticize our own tradition. We must learn from others, then come back and look at our tradition with a new horizon," Almirzanah says. "Learning from others enriches our traditions. We can be better Muslims and better Christians."

The Qur'an and Women

U.S. Catholic: What does the Qur'an [the Islamic sacred book, believed to be the word of God as Sharia Law] have to say about women?

Syafa Almirzanah: The Qur'an is very positive about women. In the story of Creation, women and men are created from the same cells, so usually scholars say that means that men and women are the same before God.

The problem is that different Muslims understand the Qur'an in different ways. Islam is not the monolithic religion people think it is, just as Christianity is not monolithic.

If you read the Bible, you cannot ignore the context. When God revealed himself, it was not in a vacuum. People who receive the revelation of God have different backgrounds, experiences, and contexts, so they respond to it differently.

The same is true in Islamic tradition. Some more traditional Muslims only focus on what's written in the text and don't pay attention to the context of the verses; other more modern Muslims look at why God revealed a particular verse and how the community at that time understood it.

The verse on polygamy, for example, says that you can marry one or two or three or four women. More fundamentalist or traditional Muslims use this verse to justify having more than one wife, but actually the verse does not stop there. It continues: "If you cannot do justice, just marry one." They ignore that crucial part of the verse. This verse was revealed after a war, and there were a lot of widows and orphans, so men were allowed to marry multiple women in order to take care of them.

You also must look at verses in relation to other verses. The Qur'an says elsewhere that even if you wanted to, you could not do justice to more than one wife. So actually Islam and the Qur'an ban polygamy. It says if you cannot do justice, just marry one woman, but it also says you can never really do justice to more than one wife.

The Historic Treatment of Women

How were women treated during the seventh century in the Arabian Peninsula at the time of Muhammad?

This is also debatable. Scholars usually compare what it was like for women before Islam and after Islam.

Most scholars say that pre-Islamic times were worse for women. They say that before Islam men could marry more than four women. A Muslim scholar will argue that Muhammad limited polygamy and advocated the ideal marriage of one man and one woman. This is progress because some say that husbands could even sell women before Islam.

But there are also many scholars who write that before Islam women's conditions were not really bad because they were free and had rights. One author says that before Islam a lot of women were involved in war and managed businesses. There is evidence of cultures where husbands came into their wives' homes when they married, and the children would belong to the women's tribe. Our Prophet's first wife was a businesswoman, and she came from a very noble tribe, though she may be the exception.

The Qur'an gives women the right to pursue an education and be involved in worldly matters.

I personally think it was almost like it is today. In certain communities where people are poor and have no access to education, of course women [might] not have the same opportunities as women who have rich families and live in an urban society. I can say that there were some good attitudes toward women before Islam, but Islam increased those good attitudes.

How did Muhammad treat his wives?

The first wife of the Prophet was a businesswoman. His youngest wife, Aisha, was a scholar and one of the interpreters of what the Prophet was saying. Because she was very close to the Prophet, a lot of people asked Aisha about what they should do in matters of love or matters of Sharia, or Muslim law. She also was involved in battle.

The Prophet didn't teach that women should just stay at home. These rules were introduced by the Prophet's companions after his death. The Qur'an gives women the right to pursue an education and be involved in worldly matters.

I think we need to get traditional Muslims to look at history, even at our Prophet's wives, and see that they were very active. Why should we now have to stay at home?

There is a verse that says men are above women, but above here does not mean women are naturally inferior. It means men are responsible for family welfare because they work out-side the home and earn money—as they [did] in Muhammad's time.

Today, a woman can go outside of the home, work, and earn money, so she has the same status as a man. She also has responsibilities for her family, so for a more modern scholar, men are not above women.

The Issue of Muhammad's Wives

How do more traditional Muslim scholars explain away the prominence of Muhammad's wives?

They say that his wives were exceptions. Most of the inter-preters of the Qur'an have been men, so there is a lot of sub-mission of women in Muslim teachings. When I was doing my graduate studies, my adviser told me that some of the in-terpreters were men who really hated women.

A lot of the misogynistic hadiths [a collection of narra-tives that recount the sayings and deeds of the Prophet Mu-hammad as well as the thing done or said in his presence which he approved] do not come from trusted sources, though.

Hadiths tell scholars about the life of the Prophet and the context of the revelations but aren't actually revelations them-selves. They are passed on through generations of people from Muhammad's contemporaries, so scholars have to make sure there is a common link back to the time of the Prophet. In order to evaluate whether the Prophet said something, we have to study the transmission of the tradition and who it came from.

We have very strict requirements to accept that a saying really came from the Prophet. Most of the misogynistic ha-diths come only from one source. These cannot be used as a resource for an edict. But some people choose the one that matches their thinking rather than the one that has the best source.

Who are other notable female figures in Islam beyond Muhammad's wives?

There are a lot. The ninth-century scholar Ibn Sa'd wrote biographies of important Islamic figures, and he had a whole book of women in Islamic history.

There are also women saints. Rabia al-Adawiyya is a very famous Sufi, or Muslim mystic. She was a pioneer for the idea of love for God in Islamic mysticism. She has a well-known prayer: "God, if I pray to you only so you do not put me in hell, just put me in hell, and if I pray to you only so I can go to paradise, don't put me in paradise, but if I pray to you only because I love you, don't hide your face from me."

Rabia is said to be in the rank of men because she was close to or one with God. A lot of Muslim women look at her as an example—the ideal mystic woman. She didn't marry, but there are a lot of women mystics who did marry. Some are the wives or daughters of male mystics. Sufi men had women teachers. A teacher of the famous Sufi Iban Arabi said, "I am his spiritual mother."

As in Christian spirituality, there are a lot of Muslim women mystics who are highly regarded. Mystics go beyond the text into the essence of the story. When you do that, every religion can meet, and men and women can meet. It is very conducive to dialogue.

There are a lot of male [Muslim] feminists who support the equal status of women, especially in Indonesia and Egypt.

Muslim Women and Feminism

Christian women sometimes struggle with male images of God. Is God thought of as male in Islam?

God is often described as having both a feminine and masculine aspect. One scholar compared it to yin and yang. In the Islamic tradition we call it Jalal and Jamal. Jalal is the might of God, and Jamal is the beauty of God. God has both of these aspects, feminine and masculine.

Yin and yang always are together, so women and men should be together. Man is not better than woman, and woman is not better than man. In Islam women and men should co-operate. Even in the Muslim Creation story, Eve is not the cause of the fall.

Still, the pronoun for God is a male pronoun, and that is a problem that feminists discuss. There are also certain verses in the Qur'an that only use a male pronoun, so Muslim feminists say that the male pronoun refers to both genders. For example, verses such as "you have to pray every day" use the male pronoun, but this doesn't mean that praying is only for males.

What does it mean to be a Muslim feminist?

Quite simply, I define it as someone who supports women's rights. There are a lot of male feminists who support the equal status of women, especially in Indonesia and Egypt. Some governments also promote equal rights.

The Status of Women in Islam

Generally, what is the status of women in the Muslim world today?

As I said, Islam isn't a monolithic religion. The place of women depends a lot on the social, political, and cultural conditions of the community. Islam in Indonesia is very different from Islam in Saudi Arabia, for example.

In Indonesia it's common for women to study and be in politics, but still there is resistance. We had a female president before our current president. When she was to be appointed president, fundamentalist groups opposed it because they said that Islam prohibited women from leading them. She became our president anyway. There are no verses that prohibit a woman from being president.

Still, many believe that women's responsibilities are domestic tasks such as cooking and taking care of children. Even my in-laws still believe that. They wouldn't let my husband cook.

When a woman's husband comes home from his job, she is supposed to serve him. But both my husband and I work outside the home, so why should I serve him? I always say, "I am not his servant. I am his wife." If I serve him on an occasion, it's not because it's my responsibility; it's because I love him.

We also have to understand there are women themselves who really believe in the fundamentalist interpretation. They believe that they should be at home and that they might have to accept being a second wife because this is what Islam teaches.

How much of that is due to religion and how much is due to culture?

I think it has to do with both. Culture is there, but certain interpretations of religion are there, too. There is a certain interpretation of Islam that says women should stay at home, not go anywhere, and take care of the family.

This is why women have to study what Islam actually teaches about women and our position. Our Prophet cooked and even sewed his clothes himself. There is nothing to be ashamed of in that.

We have to improve Muslims' understanding of the Qur'an. A lot of laypeople are Muslim because their family is Muslim, and they have never really studied their own tradition. They depend on their religious leader: Whatever he says, they will follow it. We cannot just do that; we have to know the sources of Islam ourselves.

There are a number of schools of thought for Islamic law. I was taught that you don't have to follow one of them, but the most important thing is to know why they say what they do.

Improving the Position of Women

How can women's positions in the Muslim world improve?

There are a lot of ways to improve our status, but I think the key, again, is education. Unfortunately, there are still a lot of people who do not have access to it. A lot of families in my country still pay only for boys and not girls to study if they have limited resources.

I have a brother, and my father let me go to school even to the highest levels, but that's often not the case at the university level. As a professor in Indonesia, I do see a lot of female students studying theology, though.

Why do you think some resist alternative interpretations of Islam?

I think we need more research on that. Some scholars say fundamentalism is not a purely religious movement, but is political as well, and I agree. Patriarchal culture is weakened by the Muslim feminist movement. They are strict with women because they want power.

I also think it's one way for the Muslim community to challenge modernity. When it comes to women's issues specifically, for example, fundamentalists say that a Muslim feminist is strongly influenced by the Western perspective. They criticize the feminist movement because they don't want it to be secular.

What do you as a modern Muslim make of Western feminism?

I think Muslims have to choose what is really appropriate for us and what can be applied in our tradition from Western feminism.

It does seem like Western feminists don't really need men sometimes, and I don't think Muslims should go in that direction. We have to work together. The Qur'an says that women are sustenance to their husbands, and husbands are sustenance to their wives.

Every tradition has good points and bad points. I always try to see the positive. Fundamentalists often refer to Sayyid Qutb, an Egyptian scholar who came to the United States in the late 1940s and only saw bad things—promiscuity, drugs, materialism, and so on. In his mind people in the United States were living in Jahiliyyah, the era before Islam, a state of ignorance.

Should we follow him? I think not. I came here and I saw myself what it is like in the United States. There is still much good here. We can choose to see what is good.

Muslim and Christian women should study together and go deeper into the traditions to find out what our traditions are actually saying about the position of women.

What issues do Christian and Muslim women share?

I think Muslim and Christian women have the same struggle to gain equal positions to men within our traditions. Most of the interpreters in the Catholic tradition are male, just as in Islam. That's one of the reasons they underestimate women, and there are misinterpretations of both religions.

For example, Jesus had female followers, but the Catholic tradition doesn't really consider them to be apostles. From my perspective, the women of those days were Jesus' apostles. In Islam we also have women companions to the Prophet Muhammad. But for some reason, in both cases, these women have been forgotten.

Muslim and Christian women can work together. We need to interpret verses for ourselves and criticize the old male interpretations. We should study together and go deeper into the traditions to find out what our traditions are actually saying about the position of women.

6

The Islamic Legal Code Harms Women

M.A. Khan

M.A. Khan is the editor of islam-watch.org and the author of Islamic Jihad: A Legacy of Forced Conversion, Imperialism, and Slavery.

The sharia, or the Islamic legal code, discriminates against women, causing them pain and sometimes death. In spite of this, Western countries such as the United Kingdom are allowing resident Muslims to establish sharia courts. Saudi Arabia, however, is the best place to study for examples of how sharia affects women. There, women must be strictly segregated from men and can be severely punished just for chatting with a man. Men are free to harass women as they please. The religious police, vigilantes enforcing the sharia, often inflict serious harm on women, including stoning and rape.

Islamic legal code, the Sharia, continues to [gain ground] in the West. Sharia Court, operational in Canada since 1991, was abolished in 2006 in the face of intense campaign from human rights activists. Although widely practiced by the Muslim community over the year, Sharia Court received official recognition in the U.K. for dealing with civil and some criminal cases (domestic violence, etc.) in 2007. Since some 40% of the British Muslims want the establishment of Sharia Court, with fewer of them opposed to it, this is possibly the first step in the gradual process of establishing full-fledged Islamic legal

M.A. Khan, "Living Under Sharia: The Plight of Women in Saudi Arabia," *Islam Watch*, March 14, 2009. Reproduced by permission.

codes in Britain. As Muslim immigrants in the West, from Europe to North America, show increasing support for Sharia, demand for Sharia laws in other Western countries will definitely intensify in light of this British concession.

Sharia Laws Discriminate Against Women

What people in the West must make themselves aware of is that Sharia laws are extremely discriminatory, indeed humiliating and degrading, toward non-Muslims. [They are] also highly discriminatory and humiliating toward Muslim women. . . . One may take a look at Afghanistan under the Taliban, Iran and Saudi Arabia, where Sharia laws were/are applied to varying strictness. Some 400 Girls Schools face closure in Pakistan's Swat Valley, where Sharia is poised to be instituted in weeks. In the wake of the just-concluded International Women's Day, this essay will attempt to make it clear what Sharia law means for Muslim women.

Australian Mufti Taj al-Din al-Hilali raised furor in 2006 by calling unveiled women "uncovered meat" to suggest that eighteen such white women, raped (some gang-raped) by Muslim youths in a Sydney neighborhood in 2000, actually invited the horrendous act upon themselves. Most Australians and Westerners have viewed it as utterance of a deranged ignorant cleric, not representing the Islamic creed and community. However, an investigation of the treatment of women in Saudi Arabia—the birthplace and heartland of Islam—reveals a strong Islamic rationale behind the Mufti's assertion.

Saudi Arabia, the sacred land of Islamic devotion, is the best place for evaluating the status of women in Islam, where Islamic holy laws—the Sharia, which should ideally guide Islamic societies for eternity—are implemented most rigorously amongst Islamic countries. The Saudi Basic Law says:

- *General Principle*, Article 1: "The Kingdom of Saudi Arabia is a sovereign Arab Islamic state; its religion is Islam; and its constitution is the Holy Quran [the Is-

47

lamic sacred book, believed to be the word of God as Sharia Law] and Prophet's Sunnah (traditions)"

- *System of Government*, Article 7: "Government derives its power from the Holy Quran and the Prophet's Sunnah"

- *Rights and Duties*, Article 23: "The state protects the Islamic and caters to the application of Shari'ah; it enjoins good and forbids evil and undertakes the duty of call to Islam."

Welcome to the Islamic heartland of Saudi Arabia: it's a man's world. Free Western women are truly "uncovered meat" here. Here, women almost invariably invite rapes; it's rarely [considered] a fault of men, the rapists.

When a Girls School in Saudi Arabia caught fire in 2002, the Religious Police beat the unveiled girls to prevent them from leaving the compound on blaze.

The Words of Allah

The Quran, which contains the unchanged words of the Islamic God (Allah) to guide ... Muslim life and society for eternity, commands the "wives and daughters and the women of the believers to draw their cloaks close round them (when they go abroad). That will be better, so that they may be recognized and not annoyed."

This is the last verse revealed by Allah to finalize the dress-code for Muslim women when they go out of their homes. It made veiling an obligatory eternal law of Allah. Women must be responsible and veil themselves not to attract molestation by men.

Due to changes brought about in Muslim countries during the European colonial period and pressures from the outside world (the U.N., Human Rights Groups and Western nations), most Muslim countries have relaxed this divine anti-women law. But many Arab countries apply it—Saudi Arabia being the strictest. In an ideal Islamic society, the divine laws of Allah cannot be violated under any circumstances. So, when a Girls School in Saudi Arabia caught fire in 2002, the Religious Police—the Commission for the Promotion of Virtue and Prevention of Vice—beat the unveiled girls to prevent them from leaving the compound on blaze. Unveiled women (Hilali's "uncovered meat") must not venture out, as a result, fifteen girls were burned alive to charred [corpses].

Islamic law commands strict segregation of unrelated men and women, even within the confines of home. In 2007, a group of Saudi youths caught a woman with an unrelated man in a car and gang-raped her fourteen times. The Saudi Court convicted her of violating the segregation law and sentenced to six months' jail and 200 lashes. The rapists were given light sentences of one to five years of imprisonment. When appealed, her punishment was doubled. Judge Dr. Ibrahim bin Salih al-Khudairi of the Riyadh Appeals Court later even regretted . . . not sentencing her to death.

Unchaste Behavior Is Grounds for Death

Strict Islamic societies demand that Muslim women maintain their purity, both physically and mentally. When a Saudi girl was found chatting with boys over Facebook, her father beat her before shooting [her] to death.

A woman, shot by her husband the first and second time, rejected a Social Worker's advice to file a complaint as it required the presence of her obligatory male guardian, her husband; without him, her testimony would not be accepted, whilst the Religious Police might accuse her of "mixing" with the opposite sex, a criminal offense. "The third time her husband shot her, she died of her wounds," the Social Worker told a 2008 *Human Rights Watch (HRW) Report* on Saudi Arabia.

Prophet Muhammad had set an ideal example for Islamic societies by marrying his 6-year-old niece, Aisha, at the ripe age of 52; he consummated the marriage three years later. Recently an 8-year-old Saudi girl was given to marriage by her father to a 58-year-old man. The girl's divorced mother petitioned to the court to annul the marriage. It was rejected on the grounds that only the girl can seek divorce only after reaching her puberty. She is old enough to get married, but not to seek divorce.

These are but a few examples of such incidences from the highly restrictive and secretive Saudi Kingdom that get into the media spotlight. A woman cannot go out alone, even if veiled. She must be escorted by a male relative. The HRW Report, cited above, found that Saudi women are treated as "Perpetual Minors": they are disallowed by law to study, work, travel, marry, testify in court, legalise a contract or undergo medical treatment without the assent of a close male relative—father, husband, grandfather, brother or son.

A man can divorce his wife as he wishes; Muhammad bin Laden, father of Osama, accumulated more than twenty wives—married and divorced—in his house. Since a Muslim man can only take four wives at a time, he would divorce one of the four wives, not attractive any more, to add a new one in his harem. The divorced wives stayed in his house as unwanted slaves; men are divinely sanctioned to keep [an] unlimited number of slave-concubines in Islam.

The Example of American Women in Saudi Arabia

The condition of Saudi women can be best understood from the experiences of Western women in the kingdom. American woman Monica Stowers met a young Saudi man, Nizar Radwan, at the University of Dallas and married [him] in the early 1980s. The couple moved to Saudi Arabia with their two infant [children]. Stowers was in shock; Nizar already had a wife, [whom he had] kept secret. [Stowers] protested and wanted to return to America with the kids. The Saudi Court gave the children's custody to [the] father, because the mother was an infidel, a Christian. She left Saudi Arabia alone, hoping that the U.S. Government would help in acquiring the custody of her children, which never [happened].

She returned to Saudi in 1990, met her son Rasheed at the airport, picked [up] daughter Amjad from school and headed to the U.S. Embassy, hoping to find refuge there. She had the biggest shock of her life: when she pleaded for help, the Embassy officials called two marines to kick her out. She was arrested by the Saudi police and imprisoned.

In February 2008, a 37-year old American business-woman, married mother of three, was thrown in jail by the Saudi Religious Police for sitting with a male colleague at a Starbucks.

Amjad was sodomized by her half-brother (Rasheed was also sodomized by the same half-brother, as well as by his uncle) and married off by her father at age 12. She ran away and was divorced by her husband. In 2003, Amjad, 20, along with her mother and brother (all American citizens), was living in miserable condition in an abandoned Saudi school, not permitted to leave the country. Meanwhile, the members of her father's family travel to America freely.

More Examples

Similar or worse is the story of Alia and Aisha al-Gheshayan: their Saudi father Khalid al-Gheshayan abducted them from their mother's home in Chicago in 1986 when they were 7 and 3, respectively, and smuggled to Saudi Arabia. Barred from leaving the Saudi Kingdom, as of 2002, Alia, 23, was married off to a cousin of her father, while plans were in place to marry off Aisha, 19. Their mother had lobbied with four successive State Department officials and members of Congress, but failed to get any help in bringing her daughters home.

In February 2008, a 37-year-old American businesswoman, married mother of three, was thrown in jail by the Saudi Religious Police for sitting with a male colleague at a Starbucks in Riyadh.

Such totally innocent American citizens are condemned to jail or life-long misery and horror [in the] Saudi Kingdom. The U.S. Government does not dare protest these gross violations of human rights of U.S. citizens by the Saudi authority. On the contrary, Saudi citizens, who commit grave crimes [on] American soil, are let go almost scot-free. Saudi Princess Buniah al-Saud shoved her Indonesian maid down a flight [of] stairs in Orlando (Florida) Airport in 2001. [The maid had been] repeatedly beaten previously and kept as a virtual slave. The princess was allowed to leave America while her case on charges of felony was pending. She was eventually let go by paying a $1,000 fine upon pleading guilty.

When such treatments are meted out to foreign women, including [ones] from powerful countries like America and Germany, it would not be difficult to grasp the treatment and cruelty the Saudi women suffer in the holy kingdom.

Other Foreign Women in Saudi Arabia

Dr. Sami Alrabaa, a former Muslim—who has taught in universities in Kuwait, Saudi Arabia and America—lists many harrowing tales of [suffering by] foreign women in Saudi Arabia in his book, *Karin in Saudi Arabia*.

Karin, a German woman, fell in love with a Saudi man while briefly living in Saudi Arabia. The bestial Religious Police arrested her for going on a drive downtown alone in a taxi. Upon arrest, she was raped and thrown in prison. Her German-Saudi baby son was taken away, and she was deported to Cyprus without passport and money.

Nisrin, a Bangladeshi woman, married a Saudi man. Saudis belong to an important tribe; they cannot just marry anyone, definitely not a lowly Bangladeshi. The marriage was annulled. The Religious Police raped her before deporting [her].

Luckier, young Moroccan woman Muna managed to smuggle herself and a baby [out] after one night [of] marriage with Sultan, the Crown Prince of Saudi Arabia.

Tragic are [the] stories of Mimi and Najat; they were brutally stoned to death.

Mimi, a Filipina house-maid, worked in Karin's lover's house. Denounced by his wife, she was picked up by the Religious Police and stoned to death.

When such treatments are meted out to foreign women, including [ones] from powerful countries like America and Germany, it would not be difficult to grasp the treatment and cruelty the Saudi women suffer in the holy kingdom. Here is a story of a Saudi woman. Deaf-and-[mute] Najat was arrested by the Religious Police, [who suspected her] of being a prostitute, as she waited for her brother in front of a shop-window. The Police Chief quickly passed sentence on Najat that "[She] was working as a prostitute and was caught in the very act of picking up a client. We advise that she be stoned to death. . . ." Riyadh's governor, Prince Salman, approved the punishment; Najat was publicly stoned to death [only days later].

In the introduction of his book, Alrabaa writes,

When I delivered the manuscript of this book to friends outside of Saudi Arabia, asking them to read it over, their response was uniform: they shook their heads in disbelief. Nobody in the civilized world seemed able to fathom the extent of the arbitrariness and atrocities to which victims in Saudi Arabia are subjected. To them, it was incredible. Some remarked that I was telling stories about the actions of monsters from another planet. They could not believe that any human could act as a Saudi corrupted by power does.

Men Are Free to Harass Women

In order to understand the kind of restrictive life women live in Saudi Arabia, one must read *Inside the Kingdom* by Swiss-born Carmen Bin Laden (who married a brother of Osama bin Laden and later divorced), sketching her rather liberal life there, owing to her belonging to the great bin Laden family.

But no such restrictions apply to men. Nesrine Malik, a young Muslim woman from Britain, writes of her experience of harassment in Saudi Arabia that "My sisters and I have been chased by cars full of youths many times through the streets of Riyadh, harassed through car windows and had telephone numbers expertly tossed in our laps when we had made the mistake of leaving the car window open."

Ed Hussain, a reformed British Islamist and former member of *Hizb-ut Tahrir* [a radical Islamic political movement], wrote of his experience of living in Saudi Arabia, that "In supermarkets I only had to be away from Faye [his wife] for five minutes, and Saudi men would hiss or whisper obscenities as they walked past. When Faye discussed her experiences with local women at the British Council they said: 'Welcome to Saudi Arabia.'"

He heard of a Filipino worker who had brought his new bride to live with him in Jeddah. The couple took a taxi after visiting the Balad Shopping District. On the way, the Saudi driver complained that the car was not working and asked the man to push it. As the man came out, the driver sped away with the man's wife. There was no clue about her where-abouts.

"We had heard stories of the abduction of women from taxis by sex-deprived Saudi youths. At a Saudi friend's wedding at a luxurious hotel in Jeddah, women dared not step out of their hotel rooms and walk to the banqueting hall for fear of abduction by the bodyguards of a Saudi prince who also happened to be staying there," wrote Hussain.

Prophet Muhammad's child-wife Aisha had said, "I have not seen any woman suffering as much as the believing women. . . ." The plight of Muslim women has remained the same at the birthplace, the heartland, of Islam.

7

The Qur'an Protects Women's Rights

Khalida Tanvir Syed

Khalida Tanvir Syed is a Ph.D. candidate in the Faculty of Education at the University of Alberta, in Edmonton, Alberta, Canada.

Before Islam, the treatment of women was very threatening and dangerous for women. The establishment of Islam, guided by the Qur'an, established rights for women and protected them. Women are now able to pursue a career and hold leadership positions other than leading prayers. Muslim women are also able to hold property. In addition, under the Qur'an, women cannot be forced to marry a man against their will. A woman also has the right to ask for a divorce.

Up until this point, I have focused primarily on human rights and responsibilities as described by the Qur'an [the Islamic sacred book, believed to be the word of God as Sharia Law] and Hadith [a collection of narratives that recounts the sayings and deeds of the Prophet Muhammad as well as the thing done or said in his presence which he approved], for both Muslim men and women. I now shift my focus onto the unique human rights and responsibilities that Islam has set forth for women. By referring again to the Qur'an and Hadith, I aim to clarify the misconceptions about women's rights and responsibilities in Islam.

Khalida Tanvir Syed, "Misconceptions about Human Rights and Women's Rights in Islam," *Interchange*, vol. 39, April 2008, pp. 253–56. Copyright © 2008 Springer. Part of Springer Science+Business Media. Reproduced with kind permission from Springer Science and Business Media and the author.

Pre-Islamic practices have been very threatening for women. One of the most contentious practices involved female infanticide. The Qur'an's response to female infanticide was to abolish this practice by questioning the burial of infant girls who are innocent of any crime. In addition, the Qur'an also condemned the unwelcoming attitude of some parents upon the birth of a baby girl instead of a boy by describing the attitude towards the birth of a baby girl:

> When news is brought to one of them of [the birth of] a female [child], his face darkens and he is filled with inward grief! With shame he hides himself from his people because of the bad news he has had! Shall he retain her on [sufferance and] contempt or bury her in the dust? Ah! What an evil [choice] they decide on!

But even now, the situation in some countries and cultures has not changed. The World Bank highlights in the *Millennium development goals: Promote gender equality*, that still "in some countries, infant girls are less likely to survive than infant boys because of parental discrimination and neglect—even though biologically infant girls should survive in greater numbers." Prophet Muhammad says that it is the responsibility of the parents to show kindness and justice to their daughters. He says "whosoever has a daughter does not bury her alive, does not insult her, does not favor his son over her, Allah will enter him into Paradise."

Prophet Muhammad says that it is the responsibility of the parents to show kindness and justice to their daughters.

Muslim Women May Choose Their Careers

When she grows up, a Muslim woman has the right to choose a career. "Women at the Prophet's time and after him participated with men in acts of worship, such as prayers and pilgrimage, in learning and teaching, in the marketplace, in the discussion of public issues (political life) and in the battlefield when necessary" [writes Muslim Scholar Jamal Badawi]. However, there are certain conditions for employment, and these conditions must not supersede the rulings of Islam. For example, women in the work force must maintain their modesty because it protects them from attracting unwanted attention from men. If women are not modest, they may be at risk in vulnerable social situations with men.

Fourteen hundred years ago, the Qur'an gave women the right to own property and land titles.

In Islam, there is a distinction between the roles and responsibilities of men and women. Badawi affirms that Muslim women have the right to seek employment that is both necessary and appropriate to their nature and societal needs, such as nursing, teaching, medicine, social work, business, or farming. Women can have any position of leadership except in leading prayer, and this is considered a concession to women, rather than an omission. Male leaders must go to the mosque five times a day to lead the prayers; however, women can pray at home with flexibility of time. . . .

Women in Islamic History

In Islamic history, Khadijah, a prominent business woman, employed Prophet Muhammad as an exporter and was so impressed by his honesty that she later proposed to him, and they married soon afterwards. Throughout their marriage, Khadijah not only played the role of a wife but also served as an advisor to Prophet Muhammad during the early stages of Prophethood when the Qur'an was revealed. She continuously supported Prophet Muhammad with her wisdom and acceptance of Prophet Muhammad as the chosen messenger of Allah. Other women of his time were involved in nursing, education, and cottage industries. Prophet Muhammad's caliph, Omar, appointed a woman, Um Al-Shifaa' bint Abdullah, as a market place supervisor. Fourteen hundred years ago, the Qur'an gave women the right to own property and land titles. Women are also entitled to receive marital gifts and child support. Futhermore, as a daughter, wife, sister, or mother, the woman has a right to inherit property. Owning property provides women with financial security because the money she earns is hers to keep and spend as she pleases. "From what is left by parents and those nearest related, there is a share for men and a share for women, whether the property be small or large—a determinate share" [states the Qur'an]. She is not obligated to contribute to the upkeep of the household, as that is the responsibility of the husband. The inheritance is half of a male's because females are not obligated to financially support the relatives or family, but rather the males are financially responsible for the family and the relatives.

Marriage Is Based on Mutual Love in Islam

In Islam, marriage is based on mutual love, compassion, respect, and peace. The Qur'an urges husbands to be kind to and considerate of their wives. Prophet Muhammad also instructed Muslim males to be kind to women in all relationships, such as that of a daughter, sister, niece, aunt, or mother. Badawi encourages Muslim males to practice the teachings of the Qur'an when they are engaged in a relationship with their spouse.

According to Prophet Muhammad's teachings and practices, the imposed acceptance of a marriage proposal is prohibited because it does not validate the marital contract. Badawi describes an incident of a girl who came to the Prophet Muhammad and reported that her father had forced her to marry without her consent. The Messenger of God gave her the option of accepting the marriage or invalidating it. Another version of this report states that "the girl said 'actually I accept this marriage, but I wanted to let women know that parents have no right to force a husband on them [as cited by Badawi]." These observations suggest that in Islam, females have the right to reject or select a marriage proposal and are entitled to have the freedom to choose a husband.

The [United Nations] Universal Declaration of Human Rights (1948–1998) Article 16 (2) also testifies that "marriage shall be entered into only with the free and full consent of the intending spouses" (p. 4). Divorce is permissible in Islam; however, it is not actively encouraged among the Islamic community. Some reasons for discouraging divorce include the emotional, social, and financial traumas that both parties suffer throughout their lives. Islam recognizes that two people may simply not be compatible for one another, and the woman in this scenario has a right to ask for a divorce.

8

Many Muslim Girls Endure Female Circumcision

Thomas von der Osten-Sacken and Thomas Uwer

Thomas von der Osten-Sacken and Thomas Uwer are, respectively, managing director and board member of WADI, a German-Iraqi nongovernmental organization dedicated to empowering women and achieving social equity.

Female circumcision is the practice of cutting away a girl's genitals to preserve sexual honor before marriage. It is widely prevalent throughout the Middle East and North Africa, as well as in other parts of the world. Because families often hide the practice, determining how widespread it is can be difficult. Although the Qur'an does not specifically call for female circumcision, many Muslims believe that it is a part of their religion. Girls forced to endure this procedure, without anesthesia, often suffer from infections, trauma, and sometimes death. Girls should not be mutilated in this way.

Among social activists and feminists, combating female genital mutilation (FGM) is an important policy goal. Sometimes called female circumcision or female genital cutting, FGM is the cutting of the clitoris of girls in order to curb their sexual desire and preserve their sexual honor before marriage. The practice, prevalent in some majority Muslim countries, has a tremendous cost: many girls bleed to death or die of infection. Most are traumatized. Those who survive can

Thomas von der Osten-Sacken and Thomas Uwer, "Is Female Genital Mutilation an Islamic Problem?" *Middle East Quarterly*, Winter 2007, pp. 29–36. Copyright © 2007 The Middle East Forum. Reproduced by permission.

suffer adverse health effects during marriage and pregnancy. New information from Iraqi Kurdistan raises the possibility that the problem is more prevalent in the Middle East than previously believed and that FGM is far more tied to religion than many Western academics and activists admit.

Many Muslims and academics in the West take pains to insist that the practice is not rooted in religion but rather in culture. "When one considers that the practice does not prevail and is much condemned in countries like Saudi Arabia, the center of the Islamic world, it becomes clear that the notion that it is an Islamic practice is a false one." Haseena Lockhat, a child clinical psychologist at North Warwickshire Primary Care Trust, wrote. True, FGM occurs in non-Muslim societies in Africa. And in Arab states such as Egypt, where perhaps 97 percent of girls suffer genital mutilation, both Christian Copts and Muslims are complicit.

But at the village level, those who commit the practice believe it to be religiously mandated. Religion is not only theology but also practice. And the practice is widespread throughout the Middle East. Many diplomats, international organization workers, and Arabists argue that the problem is localized to North Africa or sub-Saharan Africa, but they are wrong. The problem is pervasive throughout the Levant, the Fertile Crescent, and the Arabian Peninsula, and among many immigrants to the West from these countries. Silence on the issue is less reflective of the absence of the problem than insufficient freedom for feminists and independent civil society to raise the issue.

Female Circumcision Is Hidden

It is perhaps understandable that many diplomats and academics do not recognize the scope of the problem. Should someone wish to understand the sexual habits of Westerners, he would not face a difficult task. He could survey personal advertisements, watch talk shows, and read magazine articles explaining the best ways to enhance sexual experience, not to mention numerous scientific publications on sex and gender relations. Public knowledge of trivial and even painful matters is incumbent in Western culture. The multitude of sexual habits and gender relations represents a vital element of life in the West, much the same as the economy, politics, sports, and culture.

Rather than diminishing as countries modernize, [female circumcision] is expanding.

If, however, someone wants to study sexual relations and habits in Middle Eastern societies, it would be difficult to find comparable traces in public. Almost everything connected with sexuality and personal relations is hidden in a private sphere. Advisory books and research on sexual habits are almost nonexistent beyond comprehensive rules and prohibitions outlined by Islamic law or, in Shi'ite societies, beyond the questions and responses submitted to senior ayatollahs. Sex education is not taught at the university, let alone in any high school. Psychology remains a shadow discipline, almost absent in the eastern Middle East and only slightly more present in North Africa where more than a century of French rule offered more opportunity for it to take root. The Library of the British Psychoanalytical Society, for example, holds only one journal on psychotherapy or psychoanalysis in Arabic. Arab psychoanalyst Jihad Mazarweh gave an interview in the German weekly *Die Zeit* in which he said, "For most people, speaking about sexuality, as it happens in psychoanalysis, is almost unthinkable." It would be a mistake to interpret lack of public discussion of many sexual issues in the Middle East as indicative of a lack of problems. Rather, the silence only reflects the strength of taboo.

Female genital mutilation has been a top priority for United Nations [U.N.] agencies and nongovernmental organizations (NGOs) for almost three decades. As early as 1952, the U.N. Commission on Human Rights adopted a resolution condemning the practice. International momentum against the practice built when, in 1958, the Economic and Social Council invited the World Health Organization to study the persistence of customs subjecting girls to ritual operations. They repeated their call three years later. The 1979 Convention on the Elimination of All Forms of Discrimination against Women denounced the practice, and the 1989 Convention on the Rights of the Child identified female genital mutilation as a harmful traditional practice. According to the Demographic and Health Surveys Program, a project funded by the United States Agency for International Development to assist in undertaking medical and reproductive health surveys, FGM affects 130 million women in twenty-eight African countries. Rather than diminishing as countries modernize, FGM is expanding.

Is Female Circumcision an African Custom?

Many experts hold that female genital mutilation is an African practice. Nearly half of the FGM cases represented in official statistics occur in Egypt and Ethiopia; Sudan also records high prevalence of the practice. True, Egypt is part of the African continent but, from a cultural, historical, and political perspective, Egypt has closer ties to the Arab Middle East than to sub-Saharan Africa. Egypt was a founding member of the Arab League, and Egyptian president Gamal Abdel Nasser came to personify Arab nationalism between 1952 until his death in 1970. That FGM is so prevalent in Egypt should arouse suspicion about the practice elsewhere in the Arab world, especially given the low appreciation for women's rights in Arab societies. But most experts dismiss the connection of the practice with Islam. Instead, they explain the practice as rooted in poverty, lack of education, and superstition.

Few reports mention the existence of FGM elsewhere in the Middle East, except in passing. A UNICEF [United Nations International Children's Education Fund] report on the issue, for example, focuses on Africa and makes only passing mention of "some communities on the Red Sea coast of Yemen." UNICEF then cites reports, but no evidence, that the practice also occurs to a limited degree in Jordan, Gaza, Oman, and Iraqi Kurdistan. [A] German semigovernmental aid agency, the *Gesellschaft für Technische Zusammenarbeit*, reports that FGM is prevalent in twenty-eight African countries but only among small communities "in a few Arab and Asian countries" (e.g., Yemen, a few ethnic groups in Oman, Indonesia, and Malaysia). Some scholars have asserted that the practice does not exist at all in those countries east of the Suez Canal. Such assertions are wrong. FGM is a widespread practice in at least parts of these countries.

Midwives often perform the operation with unsterilized instruments or even broken glass and without anesthesia on girls four to twelve years old.

Female Circumcision Is Practiced Widely

[The] Latest findings from northern Iraq suggest that FGM is practiced widely in regions outside Africa. Iraqi Kurdistan is an instructive case. Traditionally, Kurdish society is agrarian. A significant part of the population lives outside cities. Women face a double-burden: they are sometimes cut off from even the most basic public services and are subject to a complex of patriarchal rules. As a result, living conditions for women are poor. Many of the freedoms and rights introduced by political leaders in Iraqi Kurdistan after the establishment of the safe-haven in 1991 [following the American-led invasion of Iraq in the first Gulf War] are, for many women, more theoretical than actual.

In early 2003, WADI, a German-Austrian NGO focusing on women's issues, started to work with mobile teams to take medical aid and social support to women in peripheral Kurdish areas such as in the Garmian region of Iraqi Kurdistan. These all-female teams consisting of a physician, a nurse, and a social worker built trust and opened doors in local communities otherwise sealed against outsiders. After more than a year of working in the area, women began to speak about FGM. Kurds in the area practice Sunna circumcision. Midwives often perform the operation with unsterilized instruments or even broken glass and without anesthesia on girls four to twelve years old. The extent of mutilation depends on the experience of the midwife and the luck of the girl. The wound is then treated with ash or mud with the girls then forced sit in a bucket of iced water. Many Kurdish girls die, and others suffer chronic pain, infection, and infertility. Many say they suffer symptoms consistent with posttraumatic stress disorder. . . .

A Very Big Problem

The discovery of widespread FGM in Iraqi Kurdistan suggests the assumption to be incorrect that FGM is primarily an African phenomenon with only marginal occurrence in the eastern Islamic world. If FGM is practiced at a rate of nearly 60 percent by Iraqi Kurds, then how prevalent is the practice in neighboring Syria, where living conditions and cultural and religious practices are comparable? According to Fran Hosken, late founder of the Women's International Network News and author of groundbreaking research on FGM in 1975, "There is little doubt that similar practices—excision, child marriage, and putting rock salt into the vagina of women after childbirth—exist in other parts of the Arabian Peninsula and around the Persian Gulf." That no firsthand medical records are available for Saudi Arabia or from any other countries in that region does not mean that these areas are free of FGM, only that the societies are not free enough to permit formal study of societal problems. That diplomats and international aid workers do not detect FGM in other societies also should not suggest that the problem does not exist. After all, FGM was prevalent in Iraqi Kurdistan for years but went undetected by the World Health Organization, UNICEF, and many other international NGOs in the region. Perhaps the most important factor enabling an NGO to uncover FGM in Iraqi Kurdistan was the existence of civil society structures and popular demand for individual rights. Such conditions simply do not exist in Syria, Saudi Arabia, or even the West Bank and Gaza, where local authorities fight to constrain individual freedoms rather than promote them.

That many women in northern Iraq—and presumably many women in Egypt—believe that the practice is rooted in religion is a factor ignored by Western universities and international organizations.

But the problem is not only that autocratic regimes tend to suppress the truth. There also must be someone in place to conduct surveys. Prior to Iraq's [2003] liberation, it was impossible to undertake independent surveys on issues such as malnutrition and infant mortality. Saddam Hussein's regime preferred to supply data to the U.N. rather than to enable others to collect their own data which might not support the conclusions the Baathist regime desired to show. The oft-cited 1999 UNICEF study claiming that U.N. sanctions had led to the deaths of 500,000 children was based on figures supplied by Saddam's regime, not an independent survey. The U.N. undertook its first reliable statistical research on the living conditions in Iraq only after liberation. Syrian, Saudi, and Iranian authorities simply do not let NGOs operate without restriction, especially when they deal with sensitive social issues.

Taboo—not social but political—is another factor under-cutting research on FGM in Arab countries. Many academics and NGO workers in the region find it objectionable to criticize the predominant Muslim or Arab cultures. They will bend over backwards to avoid the argument that FGM is rooted in Arab or Muslim cultures, even though no one argues that FGM is exclusively an Arab or Muslim problem. Statistical data from African countries indicate no clear relationship between FGM and a specific religion. Still, this does not mean that the causes of FGM do not vary across regions and that religion has no influence. As California State University anthropologist Ellen Gruenbaum has explained, "People have different and multiple reasons [for FGM] . . . For some it is a rite of passage. For others it is not. Some consider it aesthetically pleasing. For others, it is mostly related to morality or sexuality." . . .

Most studies speak of "justifications" and "rationalizations" for FGM but do not speak of causes since this could implicate Islamic rules relating to women and sexual morality. Islam is regarded as a wrong "justification," often with a citation that the Qur'an [the Islamic sacred book, believed to be the word of God as Sharia Law] does not require FGM. That many women in northern Iraq—and presumably many women in Egypt—believe that the practice is rooted in religion is a factor ignored by Western universities and international organizations. . . .

A Phenomenon of Epidemic Proportions

There are indications that FGM might be a phenomenon of epidemic proportions in the Arab Middle East. Hosken, for instance, notes that traditionally all women in the Persian Gulf region were mutilated. Arab governments refuse to address the problem. They prefer to believe that lack of statistics will enable international organizations to conclude that the problem does not exist in their jurisdictions. It is not enough to consult Islamic clerics to learn about the mutilation of girls in Islamic societies—that is like asking the cook if the guests like the meal. U.N. agencies operating in the region ignore FGM statistics, saying they have no applicable mandate to gather such data. Hosken describes it as a cartel of silence: men from countries were FGM is practiced "enjoy much influence at the U.N." and show no interest in tackling pressing social problems.

To tackle the problem, Western countries and human rights organizations need to continue to break down the wall of silence and autocracy that blights the Arab Middle East and better promote the notion of individual rights. They should withhold conclusions about the breadth of FGM and, for that matter, other social problems or political attitudes until they can conduct independent field research.

NORTH ARKANSAS COLLEGE LIBRARY
1515 Pioneer Drive
Harrison, AR 72601

9

Muslims Must Reject Violence Against Women

Mohamed Hagmagid Ali

Imam Mohamed Hagmagid Ali is the executive director of the ADAMS Center and the vice president of the Islamic Center of North America.

The murder of a well-known Buffalo, New York Muslim woman by her husband was shocking to the Muslim community. The event served to remind imams and Muslim leaders that they must not tolerate violence against women in their communities. All members of the community must support women who are suffering from abuse at the hands of their husbands. Moreover, they must help these women leave their marriages and protect them from further abuse. Under the leadership of the imams, members of the community must educate themselves and take a strong stand against domestic violence.

The Islamic Society of North America (ISNA) is saddened and shocked by the news of the loss of one of our respected sisters, Aasiya Hassan whose life was taken violently [in February, 2009 when she was beheaded by her husband]. To God we belong and to Him we return (Qur'an [the Islamic sacred book, believed to be the word of God as Sharia Law] 2:156). We pray that she finds peace in God's infinite Mercy, and our prayers and sympathies are with sister Aasiya's family. Our prayers are also with the Muslim community of Buffalo, who have been devastated by the loss of their beloved sister and the shocking nature of this incident.

Mohamed Hagmagid Ali, "Responding to the Killing of Aasiya Hassan: An Open Letter to the Leaders of American Muslim Communities," The Islamic Society of North America, isna.net, February 2009. Reproduced by permission.

A Wake-Up Call

This is a wake-up call to all of us that violence against women is real and cannot be ignored. It must be addressed collectively by every member of our community. Several times each day in America, a woman is abused or assaulted. Domestic violence is a behavior that knows no boundaries of religion, race, ethnicity, or social status. Domestic violence occurs in every community. The Muslim community is not exempt from this issue. We, the Muslim community, need to take a strong stand against domestic violence. Unfortunately, some of us ignore such problems in our community, wanting to think that it does not occur among Muslims, or we downgrade its seriousness.

Women who seek divorce from their spouses because of physical abuse should get full support from the community and not be viewed as someone who has brought shame to herself or her family.

I call upon my fellow imams [religious leaders] and community leaders to never second-guess a woman who comes to us indicating that she feels her life to be in danger. We should provide support and help to protect the victims of domestic violence by providing for them a safe place, and inform them of their rights as well as refer them to social service providers in our areas.

No Place for Abuse in Marriage

Marriage is a relationship that should be based on love, mutual respect and kindness. No one who experiences a marriage that is built on these principles would pretend that [her] life is in danger. We must respond to all complaints or reports of abuse as genuine, and we must take appropriate and immediate action to ensure the victim's safety, as well as the safety of any children that may be involved.

Women who seek divorce from their spouses because of physical abuse should get full support from the community and should not be viewed as someone who has brought shame to herself or her family. The shame is on the person who committed the act of violence or abuse. Our community needs to take a strong stand against abusive spouses. We should not make it easy for people who are known to abuse to remarry if they have already victimized someone. We should support people who work against domestic violence in our community, whether they are educators, social service providers, community leaders, or other professionals.

Our community needs to take strong stand against abusive spouses, and we should not make it easy for them to remarry if they chose a path of abusive behavior. We should support people who work against domestic violence in our community, whether they are educators or social service providers. As Allah says in the Qur'an: "O ye who believe! Stand firmly for justice, as witnesses to Allah, even as against yourselves, or your parents, or your kin, and whether it be (against) rich or poor: for Allah can best protect both. Follow not the lusts (of your hearts), lest you swerve, and if you distort (justice) or decline to do justice, verily Allah is well-acquainted with all that you do" (4:136).

Anyone who abuses their spouse should know that their business becomes the business of the community, and it is our responsibility to do something about it.

The Prophet Muhammad (peace be upon him) never hit a woman or child in his life. The purpose of marriage is to bring peace and tranquility between two people, not fear, intimidation, belittling, controlling, or demonizing. Allah the All-Mighty says in the Qur'an: "Among His signs is this, that He created for you mates from among yourselves, that ye may dwell in tranquility with them and He has put love and mercy between your (hearts): verily in that are signs for those who reflect" (30:21).

Young Men Must Be Educated

We must make it a priority to teach our young men in the community what it means to be a good husband and . . . the role the husband has as a protector of his family. The husband is not one who terrorizes or does harm and jeopardizes the safety of his family. At the same time, we must teach our young women not to accept abuse in any way, and to come forward if abuse occurs in the marriage. They must feel that they are able to inform those who are in authority and feel comfortable confiding in the imams and social workers of our communities.

Community and family members should support a woman in her decision to leave a home where her life is threatened and provide shelter and safety for her. No imam, mosque leader or social worker should suggest that she return to such a relationship and to be patient if she feels the relationship is abusive. Rather they should help and empower her to stand up for her rights and to be able to make the decision of protecting herself against her abuser without feeling she has done something wrong, regardless of the status of the abuser in the community.

A man's position in the community should not affect the imam's decision to help a woman in need. Many disasters that take place in our community could have been prevented if those being abused were heard. Domestic violence is not a private matter. Anyone who abuses their spouse should know that their business becomes the business of the community, and it is our responsibility to do something about it. She needs to tell someone and seek advice and protection.

Community leaders should also be aware that those who isolate their spouses are more likely to also be physically abusive, as isolation is in its own way a form of abuse. Some of the abusers use the abuse itself to silence the women, by telling her "If you tell people I abused you, think how people will see you, a well-known person being abused. You should keep it private."

Combating Domestic Violence

Therefore, to our sisters, we say: your honor is to live a dignified life, not to put on the face that others want to see. The way that we measure the best people among us in the community is to see how they treat their families. It is not about how much money one makes, or how much involvement they have in the community, or the name they make for themselves. Prophet Muhammad (peace be upon him) said, "The best among you are those who are best to their families."

It was a comfort for me to see a group of imams in our local community, as well as in the MANA [Muslim Alliance in North America] conference, signing a declaration promising to eradicate domestic violence in our community. Healthy marriages should be part of a curriculum within our youth programs, MSA [Muslim Students Association] conferences, and seminars, as well as part of our adult programs in our masajid [places of worship] and in our khutbahs [public prayers or addresses].

The Islamic Society of North America has done many training workshops for imams on combating domestic violence, as has the Islamic Social Service Association and Peaceful Families Project. Organizations, such as FAITH [Foundation for Appropriate and Immediate Temporary Help] Social Services in Herndon, Virginia, serve survivors of domestic violence. All of these organizations can serve as resources for those who seek to know more about the issues of domestic violence.

Faith Trust Institute, one of the largest interfaith organizations, with Peaceful Families Project has produced a DVD in which many scholars come together to address this issue. I call on my fellow imams and social workers to use this DVD for training others on the issues of domestic violence. . . .

In conclusion, Allah says in the Qur'an "Behold, Luqman said to his son by way of instruction . . . O my son! Establish regular prayer, enjoin what is just, and forbid what is wrong; and bear with patient constancy whatever betide thee; for this is firmness (of purpose) in (the conduct of) affairs" (31:17). Let us pray that Allah will help us to stand for what is right and leave what is evil and to promote healthy marriages and peaceful family environments. Let us work together to prevent domestic violence and abuse and, especially, violence against women.

10

Muslim Women Are the Victims of Honor Killings

Tarek Fatah

Tarek Fatah is the founder of the Canadian Muslim Congress.

Although the Qur'an does not call for men to kill their daugh-ters, wives, or sisters for violations of the woman's honor, these acts are more common than is apparent. In Canada, a number of girls and women have been killed for socializing with non-Muslims, not wearing a hijab, or losing their virginity before marriage. Sharia allows women to be punished or killed for en-gaging in consensual sex outside of marriage. As long as the law remains unchanged and men think of women as possessions, rather than people, such killings will continue.

Almost as soon as news broke that the murders of three Afghan-Canadian teenage sisters and their father's first wife in Kingston, [Ontario] were possible "honour killings," some in the Muslim community reacted in the most predict-able fashion: defensiveness and denial.

Instead of voicing outrage at the murders, two Muslim callers to my CFRB radio show in Toronto slammed me for raising the subject and suggested I had some hidden agenda. "This has nothing to do with Islam," said one caller, despite the fact no one on the show had, to that point, even men-tioned the word "Islam" let alone accused the religion of sanc-tioning honour killings.

Tarek Fatah, "To Cure Honour Killings 'Cancer': Islam Is Obsessed with Women's Sexu-ality," *National Post (Canada)*, July 25, 2009, p. A1. Copyright © 2009 CanWest Interac-tive Inc. and CanWest Publishing Inc. All rights reserved. Reproduced by permission of the author.

The callers were not alone. The head of the Canadian branch of the Islamic Society of North America (ISNA) told the CBC more or less the same thing—that the story was unrelated to Islam, which apparently does not permit honour killings.

Honour Killings Go On, Despite the Koran

They are both right and wrong. It is true that Islam's holy book, the Koran [the Islamic sacred book, believed to be the word of God as Sharia Law], does not sanction honour killings. But to deny the fact that many incidents of honour killings are conducted by Muslim fathers, sons and brothers, and that many victims are Muslim women, is to exercise intellectual dishonesty. At worst, it is an attempt to shut off debate.

When Mississauga, Ontario teenager Aqsa Parvez was killed, everyone from Mullahs [Muslim religious leaders] to so-called Muslim feminists claimed it was not an honour killing—even though there were allegations she had run afoul of her family for socializing with non-Muslim friends and not wearing a hijab [a head scarf worn by Muslim women, concealing hair and neck; often includes a face veil]. Critics then charged that to refer to the murder in such words was to be an anti-Muslim bigot. Humbug.

Honour killings take place because some Muslims have been convinced by their mullahs that the burden of their family's honour and their religion is vested in the virginity of their daughters and sisters.

As I said, it is true that the Koran does not sanction such murders, but man-made sharia law [Islamic law], which has been falsely imputed divine status, does allow for the killing of women if they indulge in pre-marital or extramarital consensual sex. This is precisely why so many progressive and liberal Muslims have opposed the introduction of sharia law in Canada.

There is no denying that Islam, in its contemporary expression, is obsessed with women's sexuality, and considers it a fundamental problem. The hijab, the niqab [a head scarf that covers a woman's entire face except for the eyes], the burka [a long loose garment covering the entire body with veiled holes for eyes worn in public by many Muslim women] and polygamy are all manifestations of this phobia.

The mullahs and the mosque leadership may deny their role in ensuring that Muslim women are second-class citizens within the community, but the place they reserve for women in the house of God, the Mosque, reveals their real conviction. Other than one mosque in Toronto, not a single other is willing to let Muslim women sit in the front row. They are sent to the back, or behind curtains, or pushed into basements or balconies, for they are considered not as our mothers or daughters and sisters, but as sexual triggers that may ignite male passions.

The Cancer of Honour Killings

Honour killings take place because some Muslims have been convinced by their mullahs that the burden of their family's honour and their religion is vested in the virginity of their daughters and sisters. Most mullahs acknowledge that, according to sharia law, a woman who has consensual sex with a man outside marriage deserves to be lashed in public or stoned to death by an Islamic State or an Islamic court. Don't these Islamists see how this interpretation can be taken as a license by men to take the law into their own hands?

Not until Muslim clerics and imams seriously abandon their notion about women being the possession of men will we begin to address the cancer of honour killings.

The underlying mentality is a problem in virtually all parts of the world. In October 2006, for instance, an Australian imam of Lebanese descent, the country's most senior Muslim cleric, triggered outrage when he described women who dress immodestly (in his view) as "uncovered meat" who invite sexual attacks. Sheikh Taj Al-din al-Hilali, the so-called Mufti of Australia, condemned women who, he said, "sway suggestively," wear makeup, and do not wear the hijab.

Not until the leadership of the Muslim clergy takes steps to end gender apartheid and misogyny will they be taken seriously when they say "honour killing" is not permitted by Islam.

The Koran and Men

Until 2007, only men had translated the Koran and interpreted it. That's because the very idea of a woman translating the holy book offends Islamists. Consider, for example, the reaction to the first-ever translation by a woman—Laleh Bakhtiar's *The Sublime Quran*—two years ago.

Mohammad Ashraf of the Canadian branch of the Islamic Society of North America (ISNA)—the same gentleman who this week told the CBC that there was no provision for honour killings in Islam—told *The Toronto Star* that he would not permit *The Sublime Quran* to be sold in the ISNA bookstore. "Our bookstore would not allow this kind of translation," he said. "I will consider banning it.... This woman-friendly translation will be out of line and will not fly too far."

What had Laleh Bakhtiar done to deserve the punishment of having her translation of the Koran banned from ISNA's Islamic bookstores? Her fault, in the eyes of Islamists, is that she believes the Koran does not condone spousal abuse, as claimed by Islamists.

If a woman's translation of the Koran is banned from an Islamic bookstore, what is available at such places? At one

Toronto bookstore, the title of a gaudy paperback screamed at passersby: *Women Who Deserve to Go to Hell*. The book, which is also widely available in British libraries and mosques, lists the type of women who will face eternal damnation. Among them are:

- "The Grumbler . . . the woman who complains against her husband every now and then is one of Hell."

- "The Woman Who Adorns Herself."

- "The Woman Who Apes Men, Tattoos, Cuts Hair Short and Alters Nature."

Not until the leadership of the Muslim clergy takes steps to end gender apartheid and misogyny will they be taken seriously when they say, "honour killing" is not permitted by Islam. They cannot have it both ways: proclaim women as the source of sin as well as deserving of death for consensual sex, and then claim the men who carry out the death sentence are acting against Islamic law.

11

Muslim Women's Religious Dress Should Be Banned in Public

Saira Khan

Saira Khan is a British television personality.

An increasing number of British Muslim women are wearing traditional Muslim dress, including the hijab and burqa. Although such dress is hailed as a basic religious freedom, the veil is a symbol of oppression for Muslim women. The Qur'an does not stipulate that a woman should be fully covered. Wearing the burqa and hijab isolates and limits women. It is difficult to know who among the veiled women has been forced to put it on, and who dons the burqa voluntarily. For these reasons, the dress should be banned in public.

Shopping in Harrods [an English Department store] last week [June 2009], I came across a group of women wearing black burkhas [long loose garments covering the entire body with veiled holes for eyes worn in public by many Muslim women], browsing the latest designs in the fashion department.

The irony of the situation was almost laughable. Here was a group of affluent women window shopping for designs that they would never once be able to wear in public.

Yet it's a sight that's becoming more and more commonplace. In hardline Muslim communities right across Britain,

Saira Khan, "Why I, as a British Muslim Woman, Want the Burkha Banned from Our Streets," *Mail Online*, June 24, 2009. Copyright © 2009 Solo Syndication Limited. Reproduced by permission.

the burkha and hijab [a head scarf worn by Muslim women, concealing hair and neck; often includes a face veil] are becoming the norm.

In the predominantly Muslim enclaves of Derby near my childhood home, you now see women hidden behind the full-length robe, their faces completely shielded from view. In London, I see an increasing number of young girls, aged four and five, being made to wear the hijab to school.

Shockingly, the Dickensian bone disease rickets has re-emerged in the British Muslim community because women are not getting enough vital vitamin D from sunlight because they are being consigned to life under a shroud.

The veil is simply a tool of oppression which is being used to alienate and control women under the guise of religious freedom.

Thanks to fundamentalist Muslims and 'hate' preachers working in Britain, the veiling of women is suddenly all-pervasive and promoted as a basic religious right. We are led to believe that we must live with this in the name of 'tolerance'.

The Burkha Is Oppressive

And yet, as a British Muslim woman, I abhor the practice and am calling on the Government to follow the lead of French president Nicolas Sarkozy and ban the burkha in our country.

The veil is simply a tool of oppression which is being used to alienate and control women under the guise of religious freedom.

My parents moved here from Kashmir [a disputed region between India and Pakistan] in the 1960s. They brought with them their faith and their traditions—but they also understood that they were starting a new life in a country where Islam was not the main religion.

My mother has always worn traditional Kashmiri clothes—the *salwar kameez*, a long tunic worn over trousers, and the *chador* [A full-length semi-circle of fabric, open in the front, thrown over the head, and held closed; it does not necessarily include a veil. Most common in Iran.], which is like a pashmina worn around the neck or over the hair.

When she found work in England, she adapted her dress without making a fuss. She is still very much a traditional Muslim woman, but she swims in a normal swimming costume and jogs in a tracksuit.

They wanted me to make friends at school and be able to take part in PE [physical education] lessons—not feel alienated and cut off from my peers. So at home, I wore the *salwar kameez*, while at school I wore a wore a typical English school uniform.

Now, to some fundamentalists, that made us not proper Muslims. Really?

The Burkha Is Not Required by the Koran

I have read the Koran. Nowhere in the Koran does it state that a woman's face and body must be covered in a layer of heavy black cloth. Instead, Muslim women should dress modestly, covering their arms and legs.

Many of my adult British Muslim friends cover their heads with a headscarf—and I have no problem with that.

The burkha is an entirely different matter. It is an imported Saudi Arabian tradition, and the growing number of women veiling their faces in Britain is a sign of creeping radicalisation, which is not just regressive, it is oppressive and downright dangerous.

The burkha is an extreme practice. It is never right for a woman to hide behind a veil and shut herself off from people in the community. But it is particularly wrong in Britain, where it is alien to the mainstream culture for someone to walk around wearing a mask.

The veil restricts women. It stops them achieving their full potential in all areas of their life, and it stops them communicating. It sends out a clear message: 'I do not want to be part of your society'.

Every time the burkha is debated, Muslim fundamentalists bring out all these women who say: 'It's my choice to wear this.'

Perhaps so—but what pressures have been brought to bear on them? The reality, surely, is that a lot of women are not free to choose.

[The burkha] is the weapon of radical Muslim men who want to see Sharia law on Britain's streets and would love women to be hidden, unseen and unheard.

Girls as young as four are wearing the hijab to school: that is not a freely made choice. It stops them taking part in education and reaching their potential, and the idea that tiny children need to protect their modesty is abhorrent.

And behind the closed doors of some Muslim houses, countless young women are told to wear the hijab and the veil. These are the girls who are hidden away, they are not allowed to go to university or choose who they marry. In many cases, they are kept down by the threat of violence.

The burkha is the ultimate visual symbol of female oppression. It is the weapon of radical Muslim men who want to see Sharia law on Britain's streets and would love women to be hidden, unseen and unheard. It is totally out of place in a civilised country.

Precisely because it is impossible to distinguish between the woman who is choosing to wear a burkha and the girl who has been forced to cover herself and live behind a veil, I believe it should be banned.

President [Nicolas] Sarkozy is absolutely right to say: 'If you want to live here, live like us.'

He went on to say that the burkha is not a religious sign, 'it's a sign of subservience, a sign of debasement. ... In our country, we cannot accept that women be prisoners behind a screen, cut off from all social life, deprived of all identity.'

So what should we do in Britain? For decades, Muslim fundamentalists, using the human rights laws, have been allowed to get their own way.

It is time for ministers and ordinary British Muslims to say, 'Enough is enough'. For the sake of women and children, the Government must ban the wearing of the hijab in school and the burkha in public places.

To do so is not racist, as extremists would have us believe. After all, when I go to Pakistan or Middle Eastern countries, I respect the way they live.

Women Must Unite

Two years ago, I wore a burkha for the first time for a television programme. It was the most horrid experience. It restricted the way I walked, what I saw, and how I interacted with the world.

It took away my personality. I felt alienated and like a freak. It was hot and uncomfortable, and I was unable to see behind me, exchange a smile with people, or shake hands.

If I had been forced to wear a veil, I would certainly not be free to write this article. Nor would I have run a marathon, become an aerobics teacher or set up a business.

We must unite against the radical Muslim men who love to control women.

My message to those Muslims who want to live in a Talibanised society and turn their face against Britain is this: 'If you don't like living here and don't want to integrate, then what the hell are you doing here? Why don't you just go and live in an Islamic country?'

12

A Ban on Muslim Women's Religious Dress Is Discriminatory

Human Rights Watch

Human Rights Watch is an international organization dedicated to researching and advocating for basic human rights worldwide.

In Germany, several states have banned Muslim women teachers or public employees from wearing headscarves under a law that prohibits the use and display of religious symbols in public buildings. International law guarantees an individual's freedom of religion and the right to express that religion through dress or other manifestation; German laws are in violation of these provisions. Many Muslim women must now choose between their religious beliefs or their employment. Because Christian symbols are not banned in schools, the banning of headscarves is discriminatory. German laws should be repealed or reframed so that they do not infringe on the rights of Muslim women.

In recent years there has been a debate in Germany, as in many other European countries, about how to deal with an increasingly diverse society. One of the most prominent controversies has been the wearing by some Muslim women of the headscarf, a form of religious dress that usually conceals the hair and neck. In half of Germany's states, the past five years have seen the introduction of restrictions on women wearing the headscarf in public employment, in particular in schools.

Human Rights Watch, *Discrimination in the Name of Neutrality: Headscarf Bans for Teachers and Civil Servants in Germany,* New York: Human Rights Watch, 2009. Copyright © 2009 Human Rights Watch. Reproduced by permission. http://www.hrw.org/en/node/80829/section/2.

German State Governments Control Religious Symbols

In Germany the laws and policies on the use of religious symbols in schools are the responsibility of the 16 states, not the federal government. The approach of the states toward the headscarf, and other religious symbols in schools, has varied, sometimes starkly. Eight states—Baden-Württemberg, Bavaria, Berlin, Bremen, Hesse, Lower Saxony, North Rhine-Westphalia, and Saarland—have enacted legislation and policies to prohibit teachers in public schools from wearing certain visible items of religious clothing and symbols. In two states, Hesse and Berlin, the ban is even applied more widely, covering many civil servant roles.

None of the laws banning religious symbols and dress explicitly target the headscarf. The restrictions in Bremen and Lower Saxony focus on the effect of a particular teacher's outward appearance as regards the school's ideological and religious "neutrality," but do not strictly prohibit religious clothing or symbols. Nor do they create explicit exceptions for the Christian faith or Western traditions and values. But the majority of the states with bans (Baden-Württemberg, Bavaria, Hesse, North Rhine-Westphalia, and Saarland) allow some form of exemptions for Christianity and Western cultural traditions.

The headscarf has, however, been the focus of the laws' prior parliamentary debates and explanatory documents, which have emphasized the need to recognize the Western cultural tradition shaped by Christianity (and Judaism). Furthermore, the only court cases to date involving challenges to the laws have concerned women wearing a headscarf.

The state of Berlin takes another approach. Its law, introduced in 2005, categorically bars all public school teachers (including kindergarten teachers if parents object), as well as police officers, judges, court officials, prison guards, prosecutors, and civil servants working in the justice system, from wearing visible religious or ideological symbols or garments (with the exception of small pieces of jewelry). There have been no court cases yet in Berlin under the law.

The measures effectively force women to choose between their employment and the manifestation of their religious beliefs, violating their right to freedom of religion and equal treatment.

Eight states have no specific legislation relating to religious clothing or symbols in employment. Three of those states— Brandenburg, Rhineland-Palatinate, and Schleswig-Holstein— considered but ultimately rejected such restrictions.

German Laws Violate Freedom of Religion

After examining the laws and policies in the eight German states that restrict the wearing of religious symbols, and how they are applied in practice, Human Rights Watch [an international nongovernmental organization that advocates for human rights] has found that they contravene Germany's international obligations to guarantee individuals the right to freedom of religion and equality before the law. These laws (either explicitly or in their application) discriminate against Muslim women, excluding them from teaching and other public sector employment on the basis of their faith.

Those states that ban religious clothing but still allow Christian symbols explicitly discriminate on the grounds of faith. In any event, in all eight states the ban is applied specifically against Muslim women who wear the headscarf. In practical effect, the ban also discriminates on the grounds of gender. The measures effectively force women to choose between their employment and the manifestation of their religious beliefs, violating their right to freedom of religion and equal treatment.

International human rights standards protect the rights of persons to be able to choose what they wish to wear, and in particular to be able to manifest their religious belief. Restrictions should [be implemented only] where fully justified by the state, and be the least restrictive necessary.

Banning the Headscarf Is as Bad as Requiring It

Policies and laws in countries that force women to wear the veil have repeatedly been criticized by Human Rights Watch. But laws such as in the German states, which exclude women who wear the headscarf from employment, also run foul of these international standards. These bans on wearing the headscarf in employment undercut individual autonomy and choice, privacy, and self expression, in similar ways to how they are violated in countries where women are forced to wear the headscarf.

Muslim trainee teachers have been denied subsequent employment as teachers after successful completion of their education, unless they take off their headscarves.

Such restrictions require detailed justifications, including why they are needed now when they were not required until the recent past, and why they are in practice [applied only] against Muslim women. Sufficient justifications have not been provided. While there may be legitimate grounds for some regulation of religious symbols and dress in employment for civil servants and teachers, the current wide-ranging and discriminatory restrictions adopted in German states have not been shown to be proportionate to their stated aim, and therefore amount to unlawful discrimination under international human rights law as well as violation of the rights of religion and privacy of those affected.

These regulations are not abstract concerns. The restrictions have a profound effect on women's lives, as was described by women affected who spoke to Human Rights Watch.

Teachers Are Disciplined

In those states with bans in effect, women wearing the headscarf are not permitted to work as teachers. Immediately after the new laws came into effect, teachers were asked to remove the headscarf and were reprimanded if they refused to do so, and in some cases even dismissed. Teachers, some with many years of employment, have been threatened with disciplinary action if they continue to wear the headscarf, and have been subject to disciplinary action in North Rhine-Westphalia and Baden-Württemberg.

Although those who have permanent civil servant status enjoy greater protection, they may still be removed from their teaching position and may lose their civil servant status if they continue to wear the headscarf and fail with legal challenges. Muslim trainee teachers have been denied subsequent employment as teachers after successful completion of their education, unless they take off their headscarves.

These restrictions have led some women to leave their home state or leave Germany altogether, to prolong maternity and other leave from their employment, or to leave teaching after years of studies and investment in developing their skills. Women concerned feel alienated and excluded, even though many had lived in Germany for decades or even their entire lives, or [they] are German-born converts to Islam.

Headscarf Bans Are Unnecessary

These bans are not necessary, as accommodation based on mutual respect is possible. Human Rights Watch spoke to many affected women who sought compromise and were willing to consider alternatives to the headscarf (such as large hats and untypical styles of tying the scarf), that would still allow them to comply with their religious obligations. Accommodation will require the states to . . . consult across society, act in good faith, and seek workable solutions.

Where there are concrete concerns that a teacher's conduct infringes neutrality, those concerns should be dealt with through ordinary disciplinary procedures on a case-by-case basis. Teachers should be assessed on the basis of their actions, not views imputed to them by virtue of the manifestation of their belief. Such outright and discriminatory bans as the eight states have imposed are neither justified nor necessary. . . .

German Laws Should Change

- State governments should repeal legislation on religious dress and symbols and ensure that their legislation and procedures are compatible with Germany's international human rights obligations, guaranteeing in particular that these do not discriminate on grounds of gender or religion.

- Should concrete concerns arise that a teacher's conduct infringes neutrality, those concerns should be dealt with through ordinary disciplinary procedures on a case-by-case basis.

- The Federal Anti-discrimination Office should issue public opinions assessing the discriminatory impact of state legislation restricting the headscarf and the compatibility of such legislation with the Equal Treatment Act.

- The United Nations special rapporteur [a person who presents reports] on the freedom of religion or belief should conduct a country visit to Germany to assess the compatibility of measures in place in Germany banning religious symbols and clothing in public employment with international human rights law, and issue concrete recommendations for remedying abusive policies and practices.

13

Muslim Women's Religious Dress Is a Symbol of Liberation, Not Oppression

Warina Sushil A. Jukuy

Warina Sushil A. Jukuy writes on Muslim issues for publications such as the Pinoy Press, *in the Philippines.*

A number of young Muslim women in the Philippines are upset because college authorities are banning nursing students from wearing the hijab. This is a violation of basic rights, as these women should be allowed to dress according to their religious principles. Women who choose to wear the veil do so to be liberated from attacks on their modesty. Their right to do so is guaranteed by international law. In addition, the Constitution of the Philippines guarantees freedom of religion. Therefore, women wearing the hijab are doing so as a symbol of their rights, not in response to oppression.

Some very young Muslim women approached me three weeks ago [March 2008]. They expressed their anxiety over the fact that academic policies have compelled them to take off their hijab [a head scarf worn by Muslim women, concealing hair and neck; often includes a face veil], specifically the head veil or khimar. School authorities ordered them as nursing students to take off their head veils while they are on hospital duty in the course of their RLE [related learning experience] practicum. Naturally, these veiled Muslimah are . . .

Warina Sushil A. Jukuy, "The Hijab: A Symbol of Liberation, Not Oppression," First Posted on Inside Mindanao (www.insidemindanao.com) April 25, 2008. Reproduced by permission.

apprehensive. School authorities quashed their mild protestations with the following lame, controversial, and debatable reasons: that the veil is dirty (this is either a slanderous or libelous statement); that the veil is just a cultural costume or worse a fashion ... because some Muslims wear hijab while others do not (highly fallacious); and that seeing veiled nurses on duty has traumatized hospital patients (are they running out of lucid alibi? ...)

Asking a Muslim student to take off her head veil is tantamount to asking her to strip off her unmentionables, her undergarments, or her underpants!

This brought to mind a similar hijab incident at Pilar College [a private Catholic college in Zamboanga City, Philippines]. Pilar College authorities steadfastly refused to listen to ... Muslim parents [who spoke] on behalf of their veiled daughters. [Authorities] adamantly reasoned that no one forced them to enroll their children at Pilar College and so they have to conform to school regulations just as non-Muslim OFWs [Overseas Filipino Workers, who leave their island nation to find employment abroad] have to conform to Muslim countries' legal compulsion ... to wear the veil.

The Prohibition of the Veil Shows Ignorance

Reiterating my pronouncement during the Magna Carta for Women Conference organized by [Congresswoman] Beng G. Climaco, where we lobbied for the rights for equal educational opportunity for Muslim women in the Philippines, I observed that infringement on the Muslim student's right to wear the veil is a result of profound ignorance of its divine merit and significance. Asking a Muslimah to take off her veil is not as ordinary as asking her take off her hat; or as mundane as asking her to take off her coat; or as simple as asking her to take off her shoes. In Islam, the female body, excepting the face and the hands, is considered "private parts" (awrat or juyyubihinna), and thus, the Qur'an [the Islamic sacred book, believed to be the word of God as Sharia Law] and Ahadeeth [a collection of narratives that recounts the sayings and deeds of the Prophet Muhammad as well as the thing done or said in his presence which he approved; also called "hadith"] have so decreed that it must be covered before public eyes and even in private [i.e., at home] if in the midst of prohibited or restricted males. Thus, the school authorities are unaware that asking a Muslim student to take off her head veil is tantamount to asking her to strip off her unmentionables, her undergarments, or her underpants! Thus, such action is an encroachment upon her right to privacy; it is synonymous [with] stripping her nude or [with] physical transgression.

It is clear that the State and International laws affirm the right to Islam and the right to wear the veil by Muslims is a fundamental right.

A Muslimah who wears the veil by choice, in her obedience and worship of Allah as the Supreme Being, fundamentally understands the wisdom of being covered. It is a protection of her hayya (modesty or chastity) just as the habit is as vital to a nun. How would a nun feel if one violated her habit? The hijab of a Muslimah is her shield from the penetrating bullet of evil desires . . . just as a knight cover[s] himself with an armor or a cop protect[s] himself with a bulletproof vest. How would a cop feel if he [were] deprived of his armor? One Muslimah [by] the name of Danah Quijano said, it is my life; Islam is my life! Armed with her faith in Allah, rather than disobey Allah and resolute in safeguarding her chastity, she chose to deprive herself of a nursing career and shifted to RadTech [radiology technology]. If you take off my veil, you are killing me! I understand Danah's predicament, I

[echo] her sentiments; and I know many Muslimah empathize with her. How would an astronaut feel if if he [were] deprived of his spacesuit . . . his lifeline?

Such incidents trigger [bad] memories [from] the mid-1990[s] of students being expelled from schools . . . some . . . who countered by successfully suing the French government; of one French student who staunchly fought for her Islamic aqeedah [creed] and shaved off her hair in defiance of the educational ban. She declared: "My decision to shave my head is [more] dignified than committing sins by taking off my hijab." When "religious freedom in France was restricted by a law which outlawed religious proselytizing by persons of all faiths," the French Minister of Education severely interpreted such law as banning the wearing of the hijab. Thus, he ordered the expulsion from schools of all female students who wore the hijab. President Jacques Chirac of France was even quoted to have pronounced this statement: "Wearing a veil, whether we want it or not, is a sort of aggression that is difficult for us to accept." The Roman Catholic Cardinal Jean-Marie Lustiger was alarmed that enacting a law banning the wearing of hijab in public schools would encourage an aggressive anti-religious trend. He commented: "This clumsy law risks reopening . . . a religious war."

Wearing the Veil Is a Fundamental Right

It is clear that the State and International Laws affirm the right to Islam. . . . The right to wear the veil by Muslims is a fundamental right in as much as it is a substantive right, and for these very reasons it is ordained to be inalienable. The 1987 Constitution of the Philippines declares: "The separation of Church and State shall be inviolable" (Article II, Section 6), and that, "no law shall be made respecting an establishment of religion, or prohibiting the free exercise thereof. The free exercise and enjoyment of religious profession and worship, without discrimination or preference, shall forever be allowed. No religious test shall be required for the exercise of civil or political rights" (Article III, Section 5).

Furthermore, the right to freedom of religion and the exercise of it is entrenched in Article 18 of the Universal Declaration on Human Rights and Article 18 of the International Convention on Civil and Political Rights (ICCPR). In the Philippines, Islam, as a comprehensive ad-deen or way of life, is also a deeply significant part of the cultural and ethnic identity of the Bangsamoro people. As such the Muslim Filipinos' freedom of religion is protected as both a cultural right by Article 15 of the International Covenant on Economic, Social and Cultural Rights (ICESCR) and as a right of minority groups by Article 27 of the ICCPR which states:

> In those States in which ethnic, religious or linguistic minorities exist, persons belonging to such minorities shall not be denied the right, in community with the other members of their group, to enjoy their own culture, to profess and practise their own religion, or to use their own language.

Organizations to Contact

The editors have compiled the following list of organizations concerned with the issues debated in this book. The descriptions are derived from materials provided by the organizations. All have publications or information available for interested readers. The list was compiled on the date of publication of the present volume; the information provided here may change. Readers need to remember that many organizations take several weeks or longer to respond to inquiries.

The Afghan Women's Mission
PO Box 40846, Pasadena, CA   91114-7846
(626) 676-7884
Web site: afghanwomensmission.org

According to the Afghan Women's Mission Web site, the group is moved to action by the plight of Afghan refugees, especially women and children. Their goals are to provide health care and education to Afghan refugees, and to conduct awareness campaigns on women's and human rights. The Web site provides articles and press releases, as well as significant information concerning the situation of women in Afghanistan.

The Association of Women's Rights in Development (AWID)
Toronto Office, Toronto, ON   M5T 2C7
   Canada
(416) 594-3773 • Fax: (416) 594-0330
e-mail: contact@awid.org
Web site: www.awid.org

The AWID is an international feminist organization committed to achieving gender equality, sustainable development, and women's human rights. Their mission, according to their Web site, is to strengthen the voice, impact, and influence of women's rights advocates, organizations, and movements, in order to advance the rights of women. The group's Web site offers information about their activities, links to other sources, articles, and news releases.

Islamic Society of North America (ISNA)
PO Box 38, Plainfield, IN   46168
(317) 839-8157 • Fax: (317) 839-1840
Web site: www.isna.net

The vision of the ISNA is to be an exemplary and unifying Islamic organization in North America that contributes to the betterment of the Muslim community and society at large, according to the group's Web site. Its goals include supporting Muslim communities; building good relationships with other religious communities; and developing educational, social, and outreach programs. The group's Web site includes several articles, including a section titled "Who We Are and What We Believe."

Karamah: Muslim Women Lawyers for Human Rights
PO Box 57195, Washington, DC   20037
(202) 234-7302 • Fax: (202) 234-7304
e-mail: karamah@karamah.org
Web site: www.karamah.org

Karamah is an organization of women lawyers who work for the empowerment of Muslim women within their own spiritual and cultural contexts. Its objectives are to educate Muslim women leaders to be proficient in Islamic law, to help with the development of American Muslim communities, and to be a resource for the American legal system on Islamic law. The Web site posts articles and news releases of interest and provides a comprehensive bibliography on women in Islam.

Muslim Women's Coalition
Tasneem Shamim, Executive Director, Somerset, NJ   08873
(732) 545-8833 • Fax: (732) 545-3423
e-mail: riverarc@aol.com
Web site: www.mwcoalition.org

The Muslim Women's Coalition is a nonprofit community support organization. It aims to serve as a resource for information about women in Islam. Its Web site describes various kinds of community action, outreach, and relief services, as well as providing articles and news releases.

Muslim Women's League

3010 Wilshire Blvd., Suite #519, Los Angeles, CA 90010
(626) 358-0335 • Fax: (213) 383-9674
e-mail: mwl@mwlusa.org
Web site: www.mwlusa.org

According to the group's Web site, the Muslim Women's League is a nonprofit Muslim American organization working to implement the values of Islam and thereby reclaim the status of women as free, equal, and vital contributors to society. The group's Web site provides articles and position papers, as well as an annotated recommended reading list.

Organisation of the Islamic Conference

PO Box 178, Jeddah 21411
    Kingdom of Saudi Arabia
+966 2 6900001 • Fax: +966 2 2751953
Web site: www.oic-oci.org

The Organization of the Islamic Conference is, according to its Web site, the second-largest intergovernmental organization after the United Nations. The stated mission of the organization is to be the collective voice of the Muslims of the world. The group also monitors Islamophobia around the world. The organization provides on its Web site a variety of publications, news articles, and issues, plus a comprehensive media library. Sample publications include "2008 Hate Crime Survey: Violence against Muslims" and "Combating Intolerance and Discrimination Against Muslims."

Ontario Consultants on Religious Tolerance

Box 27026, Kingston, ON K7M 8W5
    Canada

Fax: (613) 547-9015
Web site: www.religioustolerance.org

The Ontario Consultants on Religious Tolerance aim to provide a clear and unbiased description of worldwide religions, beliefs and practices. The group includes both mainstream and little known religions on its list. It has posted more than 4,800 essays on the topic. In addition, students can find essays on controversial subjects such as abortion, homosexuality, and same-sex marriage.

Women in Islam

PO Box 814, New York, NY   10037-0814
(212) 576-8875 • Fax: (212) 491-9185
e-mail: womeninislam@usa.net
Web site: www.womeninislam.org

According to the organization's Web site, Women in Islam is a group of professional and social activist Muslim women representing a broad spectrum of human rights and social justice interests. The group's goals are to increase knowledge about Islam, eliminate practices that devalue Muslim women globally, and monitor and influence programs and policies of the United Nations in order to enhance the lives of Muslim women. The group's Web site includes descriptions of its programs as well as several publications, including "Women Friendly Mosques and Community Centers: Working Together to Reclaim our Heritage," and "Timbuktu: An Empire of Knowledge: Early African Scholarship in Mali."

Women Living Under Muslim Laws (WLUML)

International Coordination Office, London   N19 5NZ
   UK
e-mail: wluml@wluml.org
Web site: wluml.org

WLUML is an international organization that provides information and support for women who are governed by laws deriving from Islam, according to the group's Web site. They focus on a number of critical issues, the most important of which is violence against women. The organization publishes a journal and a newsletter, both of which are available on its Web site. In addition, it provides a plethora of information and downloadable publications via the Resources section of its Web site.

Bibliography

Qanta Ahmed   *In the Land of Invisible Women: A Female Doctor's Journey in the Saudi Kingdom*. Chicago: Sourcebooks, Inc., 2008.

Ayaan Hiris Ali   *The Caged Virgin: An Emancipation Proclamation for Women and Islam*. New York: Free Press, 2006.

Bruce Bawer   *While Europe Slept: How Radical Islam Is Destroying the West from Within*. New York: Broadway Books, 2006.

John L. Esposito and Dalia Mogahed   *Who Speaks for Islam? What a Billion Muslims Really Think*. New York: Gallup Press, 2007.

Rana Husseini   *Murder in the Name of Honor*. Oxford, England: Oneworld Publications, 2009.

Nikki R. Keddie   *Women in the Middle East: Past and Present*. Princeton, NJ: Princeton University Press, 2007.

Bernard Lewis   *Islam: The Religion and the People*. Indianapolis, IN: Wharton Press, 2009.

Ida Lichter   *Muslim Women Reformers: Inspiring Voices against Oppression*. Amherst, NY: Prometheus Books, 2009.

Irshad Manji — *The Trouble with Islam Today: A Muslim's Call for Reform of Her Faith.* New York: St. Martin's Press, 2005.

Anna McGinty Mansson — *Becoming Muslim: Western Women's Conversions to Islam.* New York: Palgrave Macmillan, 2007.

Asra Nomani — *Standing Alone in Mecca: An American Woman's Struggle for the Soul of Islam.* San Francisco, CA: HarperOne, 2006.

Ruth Roded — *Women in Islam and the Middle East: A Reader.* London: I.B. Tauris, 2008.

Ahmed E. Souaiaia — *Contesting Justice: Women, Islam, Law and Society.* Albany, NY: State University of New York Press, 2009.

Walter H. Wagner — *Opening the Qur'an: Introducing Islam's Holy Book.* Notre Dame, IN: University of Notre Dame Press, 2007.

Bronwyn Winter — *Hijab & the Republic: Uncovering the French Headscarf Debate.* Syracuse, NY: Syracuse University Press, 2008.

Periodicals

Alaa Al Aswany — "Comment and Debate: Western Hostility to Islam Is Stoked by Double Standards and Distortion: The Political and Media Bias Is Clear," *The Guardian*, July 21, 2009.

Denise Balkissoon "Under Cover: Political or Spiritual, Oppressive or Liberating, Modest or Intimidating—Few Subjects Provoke Such Dissonant Reactions as the Veil," *Toronto Life*, Vol. 41, No. 2, February 2007.

James Copnall "Focus: Interview: 'I'm Not Afraid of Being Flogged. It Doesn't Hurt, But It Is Insulting,'" The *Observer*, August 2, 2009.

Daily Star (Beirut, Lebanon) "Violence Against Women Is Not a Tenet of the Muslim Religion," January 4, 2010.

Steven Erlanger and Souad Mekhennet "Morocco's Binding Family Code: Liberalized Law Is Praised for Empowering Women, But Some Are Left Behind," *International Herald Tribune*, August 20, 2009.

Dipesh Gadher, Abdul Taher, and Christopher Morgan "An Unholy Mix of Law and Religion," *Sunday Times*, February 10, 2008.

John Gee "Caning Case Stirs Controversy in Malaysia," *Washington Report on Middle East Affairs*, Vol. 28, No. 8, November 2009.

Sheeva J. Ghassemi "Making Space for Islam in the Workplace," *National Law Journal*, September 28, 2009.

Roba Gibia — "Sudan Is Still Living in the Era of Arabs Before Islam!" *Sudan Tribune*, August 10, 2009.

Andrew Gilligan — "Sharia Helps Women, Says Obama Adviser," *Daily Telegraph*, October 9, 2009.

Tawfik Hamid — "Bowing to Shariah Stokes Radical Islam's Fire," *Newsmax*, December 10, 2009.

Nicholas D. Kristof — "Religion and Women," *International Herald Tribune*, January 12, 2010.

Rod Liddle — "Sarkozy's Burqa Ban Panders to Racism, Not Feminism," *Spectator*, Vol. 310, No. 9435, June 27, 2009.

Jan M. Olsen — "Denmark Urges Full Use of Rules Limiting Face Veil," *The Washington Post*, January 28, 2010.

Leanie Reid — "Right to Rape: Is That What We're Fighting For? Afghan's President's Collusion with Conservatives Is Pragmatism over Ideology, But We May Have to Live with It for Now," *The (London) Times*, August 18, 2009.

Christina Hoff Sommers — "The Subjection of Islamic Women and the Fecklessness of American Feminism," *Weekly Standard*, Vol. 12, No. 34, May 21, 2007.

Jerome Taylor — "Forced Marriage Victims' Calls Going Unanswered," *The Independent*, January 28, 2010.

Robin Wright   "Islam's Soft Revolution: Dalia Ziada's Human Rights Activism, and Being A Muslim and a Woman in Iran," *Time*, Vol. 173, No. 12, March 30, 2009.

Index